DRAG

THE BASICS

Mark Edward and Chris Greenough

Routledge
Taylor & Francis Group

LONDON AND NEW YORK

Designed cover image: Berezka_Klo, Getty Images

First published 2026
by Routledge
4 Park Square, Milton Park, Abingdon, Oxon OX14 4RN

and by Routledge
605 Third Avenue, New York, NY 10158

Routledge is an imprint of the Taylor & Francis Group, an informa business

British Library Cataloguing-in-Publication Data
A catalogue record for this book is available from the British Library

Library of Congress Cataloging-in-Publication Data
Names: Edward, Mark (Professor of performance arts) author |
Greenough, Chris, 1979- author
Title: Drag : the basics / Mark Edward and Chris Greenough.
Description: London ; New York : Routledge, 2025. | Series: The basics |
Includes bibliographical references and index.
Identifiers: LCCN 2025030629 (print) | LCCN 2025030630 (ebook) |
ISBN 9781032556901 hardback | ISBN 9781032279466 paperback |
ISBN 9781003431800 ebook
Subjects: LCSH: Drag performance--History | Cross-dressing--History |
Female impersonators--History | Male impersonators--History
Classification: LCC PN1969.D73 E39 2026 (print) | LCC PN1969.D73 (ebook)
LC record available at https://lccn.loc.gov/2025030629
LC ebook record available at https://lccn.loc.gov/2025030630

ISBN: 9781032556901 (hbk)
ISBN: 9781032279466 (pbk)
ISBN: 9781003431800 (ebk)

DOI: 10.4324/9781003431800

Typeset in Bembo
by KnowledgeWorks Global Ltd.

'The time span, geographical spread and epistemology of the drag practices examined in this book are stunning: from Japanese Kabuki and Noh theatre to Thai kathoey cabaret shows, from Brazilian drag queen Pabllo Vittar to Lebanese Grand Ball drag nights, from drag pageantry in South Africa to the annual Koovagam festival in India. This is a timely book with a truly global vision.'

Hongwei Bao, author of *Contemporary Chinese Queer Performance* (Routledge, 2023).

'It's common to claim that "Drag is political!" *Drag: The Basics* substantiates this mundane assertion by staging the artform's relationship to major political phenomena: AIDS activism, media censorship, colonial law, and global warfare. Drag, we learn, is complicit in racism and ableism, but it is also a tool to critique apartheid and demand trans liberation. This book is comprehensive in its global and temporal review, and will serve as a critical foundation to all future drag writing. Infinitely teachable in the classroom and pleasurable to read at the coffeeshop, *Drag: The Basics* will teach even the most seasoned scholars and performers a thing or three.'

Kareem Khubchandani, Associate Professor of Theatre, Dance, and Performance Studies at Tufts University, USA.

'*Drag: The Basics* provides a scholarly yet accessible account of drag's history, relationship with gender performativity, and its place in media and celebrity cultures. This is an essential book for anyone interested in queer studies, gender studies and celebrity studies. We are in a time in which widespread public attention on drag culture is increasing, both in ways which celebrate it among mainstream audiences and, simultaneously, denounce it as a dangerous attack on social and gender norms. There has never been a more urgent need for a book such as this which expertly, clearly and confidently outlines the key issues. Mark Edward and Chris Greenough have provided what is undoubtedly the best critical primer on the topic to date. By spanning a wide array of regions from India to Aotearoa New Zealand, and from Canada to China, as well as key temporal instances in both history and contemporary society, from #MeToo to the experience of drag during the COVID-19 pandemic, the authors demonstrate the global appeal of this creative and cultural form, and outline the reasons why it is now sometimes controversial but also much loved.'

Rob Cover, Professor of Digital Communication at RMIT University, Melbourne, Australia.

'"What is drag?" ask Edward and Greenough in the very first line of this book. Admitting that there is no simple answer, they nevertheless go on to capture the extravagance, complexity, and troubling (in multiple senses of the word) nature of drag. From history to theory and practice to media portrayals, they cover it all, enlivening the narrative with imagery and metaphor drawn from the glittery world of drag performance.'

Leila J. Rupp, Distinguished Professor of Feminist Studies, University of California, USA.

'This engaging, accessible book emphasises drag's resistance to neat classifications. It delves into theoretical accounts of drag performance, drag histories, herstories, and theirstories, and international case studies. While showing the necessity of understanding drag in an intersectional way, the book does not shy away from addressing problematic dimensions of particular performances and scenes. This brings us a fuller, more nuanced understanding of the ways drag interacts with power, privilege, and oppression. The book also provides useful updates and insights into the shifts in (some) drag subcultures during and following the COVID pandemic, allowing us to show how the mediums through which drag is performed and transmitted change and reshape its practice.'

Ash Kayte Stokoe, author of *Reframing Drag: Beyond Subversion and the Status Quo* (Routledge, 2019).

'It is not contentious to say that drag is having a moment. And like all moments, we attempt to box drag up in its more spectacular, commercial guise in order to understand it. But as Mark Edward and Chris Greenough so delightfully and comprehensively show, drag resists any attempts to fix it into a universal practice or context. Edward and Greenough take us on a journey across the world, and over time, to showcase drag's vagaries, contradictions and complexities. This book on drag basics is hardly that; instead, it is a wonderful showcasing of everything we love, hate and ponder over. This book is part of that moment that drag is having.'

Kerryn Drysdale, Senior Research Fellow at the Centre for Social Research in Health at UNSW Sydney, Australia.

I0023492

DRAG

THE BASICS

Drag: The Basics offers a concise, critical, and intersectional exploration of drag performance through its rich histories, theories, practices, and politics across global contexts.

Through sharp analysis and compelling case studies, this accessible volume delves into drag's complex relationships with race, gender, sexuality, class, disability, and media representation. The book traces drag's transformative journey from countercultural expression to mainstream phenomenon, examining its role in protest, activism, and artistic innovation, while providing fresh insights that go beyond surface-level understanding.

Drag: The Basics is ideal for students and scholars in performance studies, gender theory, queer studies, and cultural history, as well as performers and curious enthusiasts seeking deeper engagement with drag cultures beyond make-up and glitter.

Mark Edward is a performer, artist, and independent scholar.

Chris Greenough is professor of social sciences at Edge Hill University, UK.

The Basics Series

The Basics is a highly successful series of accessible guidebooks which provide an overview of the fundamental principles of a subject area in a jargon-free and undaunting format.

Intended for students approaching a subject for the first time, the books both introduce the essentials of a subject and provide an ideal springboard for further study. With over 50 titles spanning subjects from artificial intelligence (AI) to women's studies, *The Basics* are an ideal starting point for students seeking to understand a subject area.

Each text comes with recommendations for further study and gradually introduces the complexities and nuances within a subject.

ACTING HEIGHTENED TEXT
CATHERINE WEIDNER

LIBERTARIANISM
JESSICA FLANIGAN AND CHRISTOPHER FREIMAN

CLOSE READING (SECOND EDITION)
DAVID GREENHAM

FEMINISM
RENEE HEBERLE

MINDFULNESS
SOPHIE SANSOM, DAVID SHANNON, AND TARAVAJRA

URBAN DESIGN
TIM HEATH AND FLORIAN WIEDMANN

PUBLIC RELATIONS (SECOND EDITION)
DEBORAH SILVERMAN

EDUCATION STUDIES
CATHERINE SIMON

DRAG
MARK EDWARD AND CHRIS GREENOUGH

For more information about this series, please visit: www.routledge.com/The-Basics/book-series/B

For Pat, Sylvia, and Valerie

CONTENTS

ACKNOWLEDGEMENTS

Thank you to Jodie Collins and colleagues at Routledge for their patience with the project, which was interrupted by ill-health, redundancy, and bereavement. We also wish to thank Hamish Ironside for his work with the copy editing, and the anonymous peer reviewers.

Chris would like to thank a number of friends and colleagues who have cheered him on this past year particularly: Caroline Blyth, Vicky Bosward, Deryn Guest, Seán Henry, Allison Moore, Justine Smith, Johanna Stiebert, Barbara Thiede, and Helen Thomas. He thanks his family; his dad, brothers Frank, Bernie and Neil, and sister Tricia. He is grateful to work with such supportive colleagues in the Department of History, Geography and Social Sciences at Edge Hill University, and especially enjoyed conversations with Giles Briscoe and Char Binns.

Mark thanks his sisters, Val and Liz, and brother, Barry, for all their love and support. He is most grateful to Jan Newton (Miss Balmer) for being a change agent during his school days. He is appreciative of the drag queens from Henry Africa's in Wigan in the 1980s, especially his long-time close friend (and drag mentor) Chris D'Bray, who helped to fuel his passion for drag.

Mark would like to pay tribute to the memories of Darren Wilson for his childhood friendship, Gary Bradshaw for his fierceness in the face of homophobic adversity and Christine Leckie for putting him onto the path of fabulousness. Thanks also to Paul Derbyshire, Gary Everett, and drag partner-in-academia, Stephen Farrier.

During the writing of this project Mark's mum, Sylvia, died. She was his number one fan and showed him much love and support throughout his life, no matter how outrageous he was. She would have been proud of this book. Mark would also like to pay homage to his late dad, Joseph, and sister, Denise. Denise introduced him to platform boots, sticky block mascara, women in suits, and men in make-up.

Both Mark and Chris would like to thank Cathy Butterworth, Nikki Craske, Peter Hall, Carol Lawrence, Jill and Kevin Lawrence, and Pat Meadow for their friendship and encouragement. Thanks to Yulu, Mylo, Hulot, Hylda, and Romeo for their company.

Finally, Mark would like to thank Chris for his productivity and organisational skills. Chris would like to thank Mark for his irreverent nature and his ability to make him laugh.

'Together we can accomplish more than we can do alone.'

INTRODUCTION

DRAG'S DEFIANCE OF DEFINITIONS

What is drag? It is a good question, but one with no simple answer. Drag refuses a clear and definitive definition, and rightly so. Historically, socially, politically, and culturally, drag has evolved, bent, flexed, and resisted neat categorisation. To pair the word 'drag' with 'basic' is almost a contradiction in terms! In its slang usage, the word 'basic' can be used in a derogatory way, to signify something unoriginal or conformist. As will be seen throughout the pages of this book, drag is anything but basic. It has been a site of creativity, disruption, activism, protest, and performance. At different moments, drag has been popular, marginalised, politicised, and commercialised. This book is about tracing, theorising, and questioning these shifting perspectives. Its simple aim is to offer a critical yet accessible introduction to drag's complex histories, theories, issues, and practices.

At the outset, it is important to state that drag is anything but straight, and it is certainly not a monolith. Drag has many faces and many meanings, depending on context, time, and space. Definitions that attempt to fix what drag *is* inevitably fall short. Historically, drag has often been framed through the narrow lens of cross-dressing for performance, typically seen in binary terms as a man dressing as a woman, or a woman dressing as a man. Early writings such as E. Carlton Winford's *Femme Mimics* (1954) and Roger Baker's *Drag: A History of Female Impersonation on the Stage* (1968) used terms and conceptual frames that, while accepted and used at the time, now feel historically situated and limited, because they are shaped by the

DOI: 10.4324/9781003431800-1

contexts in which they were written. Their works, though pivotal, were clearly Western-centric, and binary in outlook. With contemporary eyes, we are able to evaluate how far drag has come, and interrogate drag histories at the intersections of race, class, disability, sexuality, and colonial histories to form a contemporary collage of drag (see Chapter 2).

More critical definitions of drag can be found in a range of academic scholarship on drag, given the explosion of interest in drag in both popular culture and in the academy. Jack Halberstam discusses drag kings as 'a female (usually) who dressed up in recognizably male costume and performs theatrically in that costume' (1998: 232). Felix Le Freak in their book *Serving Face* says 'drag is a form of creative self-expression that uses costume, makeup, and/or performance to play with traditional notions of gender. Where society has said, 'This is a man and this is a woman', drag has stuck out its tongue and brazenly answered, No!' (Le Freak 2020: 11). Judith Lorber writes about the performance aspects of drag, stating in her preface to Steven Schacht and Lisa Underwood's editorial volume, *The Drag Queen Anthology,* 'drag's core elements are performance and parody. Drag exaggerates gendered dress and mannerisms with enough little incongruities to show "otherness" of the drag artist' (Lorber 2004: xv). Lorber goes on to mention how drag plays out in parody and audience responses: 'The joke is that a man can be a woman or a woman a man convincingly enough that the "unmasking" – or "unwigging" – at the end of the performance gives pleasurable *frisson* and evokes laughter' (2004: xv).

More recently, drag scholar Stephen Farrier says drag moves beyond what is in front of our eyes in a drag performance, and defines drag through its own histories that precede a performance. He argues, 'drag can be seen as a performance through which many enactments take place: those that transmit histories, generate community, stimulate desire and act as a site for the contestation of politics in the community' (Farrier 2021: 58). Kareem Khubchandani highlights the reach and impact drag has on its communities, 'drag has an inherent capacity to evoke pleasure, politics, physical rigor, and awe. Even passively consuming an unabashedly gender-bending drag performance can feel rebellious, since we still live in a conservative and normative world where gender binarism, hetero-patriarchy, queerphobia and sexism remain firmly entrenched' (Khubchandani 2023: 3).

Drag is a complex affair with a patchy and evolutionary history. Performance artist and activist Penny Arcade discusses this development and progression:

> I first witnessed drag on the, then, mean streets of New York as a courageous action. An attempt at a fuller expression of self and self-defined identity. Then I watched as drag became a performance of identity and politics and, finally, I have watched drag become an art form.
>
> (Arcade 2021: xxv)

Ultimately, however, drag dodges a paint ball of definitive definition and often runs riot among the undefinable. Ash Katye Stokoe is right in noting this, as they state, 'drag resists a straightforward definition. Although many people – including theorists and fans – have strong ideas about drag and its impact, these ideas frequently contradict each other' (Stokoe 2019: 1). Drag is dynamic and ever evolving. The shape shifting of the performance form has been part of its appeal and survival. Therefore, drag's resistance to neat, clear definitions is simply part of its creativity.

In this introduction and in true drag style, we set out our foundation first. At the heart of our perspective on drag, we acknowledge how drag today encompasses a range of identities and practices. These are multiple and can include, but are not limited to, queens, kings, genderqueer and non-binary performers, and many others who play with, parody, subvert, or celebrate gender through performance. In tracing drag's cultural impact, we highlight how it is simultaneously about glamour and grit, visibility and invisibility, tradition and transformation, and all the spaces in between such binary terms!

Yet drag is not immune from critique, and we caution that drag should not be romanticised. Accordingly, we seek to call out how drag can sometimes reproduce the very hierarchies it seeks to disrupt, particularly in relation to race, gender, body conformity, and access (see Chapter 2). Drag is therefore messy, contradictory, and problematic. This book seeks to shine light on this complexity, without reducing drag to easy slogans or naïve assumptions.

This book is aimed at drag performers, fans, as well as students, scholars, practitioners, and general readers interested in LGBTQ+

histories, performance studies, gender studies, queer theory, media studies, cultural studies, and activist art practices. It provides a critical but accessible exploration of drag's histories, theories, and contemporary practices, without assuming prior specialist knowledge. Additionally, we do not seek to dilute or simplify the serious complexities and issues involved in drag. The approach taken throughout is intersectional, interdisciplinary, and interrogative.

STRUCTURE OF THE BOOK

Chapter 1 offers a critical history and herstory of drag, from ancient cross-gender performances through to contemporary drag practices. It acknowledges from the outset that tracing drag histories is fraught with gaps, silences, and fragmentations. LGBTQ+ lives and performances have often been erased from official histories due to legal, religious, and social persecution. With this in mind, this chapter works with fragments, archives, and a quest for queer traces. The chapter explores a vast range of historical periods: ancient rituals, Greek and Roman theatre, Japanese Noh and Kabuki traditions, Elizabethan and Restoration theatre, molly houses, music halls, Weimar cabarets, and wartime revues. What emerges from such a vast history is drag's resilience and adaptability through different periods and cultural contexts. Throughout its pasts, drag has always had a survival strategy, negotiating its way through social expectations, legal restrictions, and cultural anxieties around its form.

Chapter 2 moves from historical narratives to theoretical frameworks. It explores how drag has been theorised through feminist perspectives, queer theory, gender performativity, and intersectionality. The chapter traces the development of feminist critiques of patriarchy and heteronormativity, the emergence of queer theory's challenges to fixed sexual and gender identities, and Judith Butler's work on gender performativity. For Butler, drag is seen as a critical site that exposes the performative and socially constructed nature of gender itself. However, the chapter is careful not to present theory as detached from practice. Instead, it highlights how theoretical debates emerge from, (or, indeed, *ought to emerge from*), lived experiences, activist movements, and creative practices. Beyond these key ideas, the chapter explores pressing issues within drag today, including misogyny within drag cultures, the underrepresentation of drag kings and non-binary performers, racial inequalities, class, disability exclusion, and the complex entanglement of drag and trans politics. The final part of the chapter examines drag's activist potential, detailing case studies where drag intersects with activism around issues such as LGBTQ+ rights, gender-based violence, religion, mental health advocacy, sexual health, and climate justice.

Chapter 3 focuses on drag and the media. It critically examines how drag is portrayed in television and film, on radio, and across digital platforms. It traces drag's appearances from early TV comedy sketches to mainstream global phenomena such as *RuPaul's Drag Race*. The chapter explores how media shapes representations of drag and is shaped by drag in various ways; sometimes the media expands drag's reach and activist potential, sometimes it dilutes its subversive edges in favour of commercial palatability. Case studies include drag's intersections with colonial histories, capitalism, and community-based media projects. While earlier representations of drag in the media focus on drag queens (and largely still do), attention here is also given to a broader constellation of performers often erased from mainstream narratives. The chapter insists on resisting narrow framings found in formulaic TV shows, and highlights alternative drag scenes that resist the commercial mainstream.

3 Cs OF DRAG: CREATIVITY, CELEBRATION, AND CRITICALITY

Throughout this book, we offer three approaches to our discussion of drag: creativity, celebration and criticality; the 3 Cs. First, the notion of 'creativity' refers to how drag is often interpreted and appreciated for its performance and aesthetic artistry. Despite creativity being an oft-used term to describe drag, we seek to delve a little deeper into what creativity means in drag terms. Jamie Campbell Naidoo (2018) notes how drag story time is not just creative in the events, tasks and stories told, but how it presents gender creativity. This is a key component of drag's creative potential: to persist in disrupting binary gender. As an art form, drag is abundantly creative: there is a do-it-yourself spirit and energy in which personas are self-fashioned, self-created, and born into existence. The use of fashion, costume, make-up, wigs, prosthetics and other aesthetics are creatively applied to have visual impact. This process is often reduced to being labelled as a 'look', but it is so much more. It is the building of identity and artistry. Beyond the visuality, drag demonstrates physical and auditory creativity through movement and sound. The use (and absence) of voice through narratives, comedy, live singing, and lip-syncing all point to creative, sensory methods. As will be seen in Chapters 1 and 3 specifically, drag does not stand still. It moves with the times and embraces advancements in digital technology to add to its creative arsenal.

Second, our approach to drag is celebratory. Throughout the chapters, we trace the survival of drag as a queer art form and celebrate its ability to shape shift into various forms and platforms in order to maintain its presence. Drag survives and thrives. Its popularity as a form of entertainment is undoubtable, but this comes through a long history of struggle and resistance (see Chapter 1). Readers in countries in which LGBTQ+ people have protected rights in law do not need reminding that these rights do not signify that all prejudice, discrimination and violence have been erased in those countries. Moreover, a quick glance over land borders on this small planet indicates that there is still much work to do in the advancement of rights for LGBTQ+ people across the globe (see Chapter 2).

Lastly, and most importantly, we are critical of drag. While we care deeply about drag, we do not seek to romanticise the art form. Consequently, we do not shy away from difficult discussions where drag has been problematic. In the academic sense, being critical does not mean reading or roasting the art form, by tearing it to shreds. Criticality means being able to offer balanced, evaluated, and informed perspectives on drag, juxtaposing positive and negative elements. Here, criticality is less about opinions, feelings and views, but it is grounded in evidence to support the arguments and cases made. This is essential for all entertainment industries, which have lasting legacies of questions of inclusion, injustices and inequalities.

In the spirit of criticality, we are self-reflective in the limitations of our endeavour to provide a concise overview of drag. The first is that necessary decisions have been made to offer content that is detailed enough to give an overview, but we hope such content allows a motivated reader to go and explore further resources for themselves, should they seek a deeper dive. Drag's popularity means there are a number of texts available, aimed at both popular and academic audiences. The plethora of websites, online videos, documentaries and other digital footage offers a wealth of resources about drag. What we offer as authors in this book is an overview of the complexity of drag; we simply attempt to capture drag at a very specific moment in its history and evolution. Future ideas and revelations will undoubtedly shift some of the contemporary perspectives we have on drag.

One further challenge that we have fought hard to resist throughout this book is a complete text that focuses exclusively on white, Western perspectives. This has required some navigation and negotiation in many ways: as the text is written in English and drag's popularity in the UK, USA, Australasia, and Canada has been an abundant source of case studies and examples, as the reader will see. Yet, our research also draws from examples of drag in specific global contexts, including case studies from Asia, Africa and Latin America. As white male scholars in the UK, we seek to work with intersectional approaches and we literally see the white in our own eyes. Here, we are reminded of Stuart Hall's significant essay, 'The Whites of Their Eyes: Racist Ideologies and the Media' (1981). Hall offers critical insights and encourages white academics to reflect on their position in media studies. This is an essential invitation for those of us who are concerned particularly with examining the intersections of race, representation, and power in drag. For white academics, this involves acknowledging how our perspectives and interpretations are influenced by our racial and cultural backgrounds. Positionality and context are key: while we have privilege in one area, we may be marginalised in others. We are aware of some of our own intersectional categories: disability, chronic illness, fatness, neurodivergence, working-class backgrounds, queerness. For drag studies specifically, there is still much more urgent work to do in this regard. Hall's essay serves as a call to action for academics to engage with media content critically, urging readers to question both the messages conveyed and also the mechanisms through which certain ideologies are maintained and others are suppressed. In terms of race and ethnicity, we have therefore sought, where possible, to seek out and amplify narratives that resist the colonisation of drag. Chapter 2 specifically calls for an interrogation of intersectionality and drag. On this point, an essential read and companion text to ours is Kareem Khubchandani's pivotal text, *Decolonize Drag* (2023).

A final reflection relates to the coherency of this book. The three chapters are formed to ensure a clear, narrative structure to the volume, with the aim of presenting ideas and discussions in a fluent and logical way. Each chapter, indeed each section, is also designed to be read alone, should a reader wish to focus on one particular theme. Accordingly, the content across the book is complementary: an idea in one chapter may be cross linked to a discussion in another.

Across the three main chapters, certain threads run consistently: (1) the refusal of neat definitions; (2) the focus on historical, cultural, and contextual specificity; and (3) the value of intersectional approaches. If drag has taught us anything, it is that the categories we inhabit are never fixed or final. Drag embraces identities that are fluid, performative, and resistant. So what began as an act of courageous self-expression, parody, comedy or performance, drag has now emerged as a complex, political and diverse art form. This book follows that journey, celebrating drag, without ignoring its contradictions and complexities.

Welcome to the stage.

REFERENCES

Arcade, P. (2021). 'Foreword'. In Edward, M. & Farrier, S. (eds), *Drag Histories, Herstories and Hairstories: Drag in a Changing Scene Volume 2*, xxi–xxv. London: Bloomsbury.

Baker, R. (1968). *Drag: A History of Female Impersonation on the Stage*. London: Triton.

Farrier, S. (2021). 'Kinging the Stage: Male Impersonators and Drag Kings, Exploring Shared Historical Narratives'. In Edward, M. & Farrier, S. (eds), *Drag Histories, Herstories and Hairstories: Drag in a Changing Scene Volume 2*, 57–68. London: Bloomsbury.

Halberstam, J. (1998). *Female Masculinity*. Durham, NC: Duke University Press.

Hall, S. (1981). 'The Whites of Their Eyes: Racist Ideologies and the Media'. In Bridges, G. & Brunt, R. (eds), *Silver Linings: Some Strategies for the Eighties*, 28–52. London: Lawrence and Wishart.

Khubchandani, K. (2023). *Decolonize Drag*. New York: OR Books.

Le Freak, F. (2020). *Serving Face: Lessons on Poise and (Dis)grace from the World of Drag*. London: DK Publishing.

Lorber, J. (2004). 'Preface' in Schacht, S. P. & Underwood, L. (eds), *The Drag Queen Anthology: The Absolutely Fabulous but Flawless Customary World of Female Impersonators*, xv–xvi. New York: Routledge.

Naidoo, J. C. (2018). 'A Rainbow of Creativity: Exploring Drag Queen Storytimes and Gender Creative Programming in Public Libraries', *Children and Libraries*, 16(4), 12–22.

Stokoe, A. K. (2019). *Reframing Drag: Beyond Subversion and the Status Quo*. London: Routledge.

Winford, C. E. (1954). *Femme Mimics*. Dallas, TX: Winford Company.

1

A HISTORY/HERSTORY OF DRAG

INTRODUCTION

Unless you have been orbiting in space for many years and you have had no communication with planet Earth, then you are going to be fully aware of the huge visibility that drag forms have been given in people's lives right now. However, this has not always been the case. If we take a stiletto hop, skip and a jump back in time, there is documented evidence that signposts us to a myriad of histories/herstories that narrate tales of celebration, liberation, secretive or subcultural practices, discrimination, and even death. These historical accounts show how there have been numerous rises and falls in drag. So, strike a pose and let us shimmy back into drag pasts.

Tracing drag histories/herstories is entirely problematic, given that the identities we know as LGBTQ+ were illegal in a number of contexts in the past. This meant that people had to make deliberate, conscious efforts not to leave a trace about their nonconforming gender and sexual identities, and drag is no exception to this. With this in mind, there is no concise, full account of drag history/herstory available to us. Drag historians work with a gaydar or a whiff of lavender in order to elicit drag pasts. Queer histories have often not been documented, have been self-censored or erased from history precisely due to the illegality of homosexuality, alongside prejudice and discrimination against LGBTQ+ lives. Accordingly, this chapter offers a brief overview of the histories/herstories of drag that are available to us and can be interpreted through piecing together the fragments and sequins of drag pasts.

DOI: 10.4324/9781003431800-2

In this chapter we trace drag as a shape-shifter. Drag is a performance art with a survival strategy that has endured throughout the ages. From ancient stages to pandemic live streams, drag has worn many faces and costumes, but the overarching element has always been resistance dressed up and disguised as performance. The chapter opens with drag's earliest traces. Then we move to more recognisably theatrical forms, such as Elizabethan boys in wigs, and Japanese Edo-period *onnagata*. In the twentieth century, when Weimar cabarets bloomed in Germany, drag spaces were destroyed. Still, at this time, drag persisted and re-emerged, disguised in trench cabarets, pub shows, and late-night revues. Since then in Britain, America, South Africa, India, and beyond, drag performers re-adjust their wigs and carry on. This chapter does not pretend to be complete. Instead, it reads like short case study accounts, sketching out various forms of drag from different contexts.

There are three contextual limitations to this overview. First, we must pay attention to how terminology used to conceptualise or talk about drag has evolved over time. Some terms that seem antiquated, or are loaded with political importance today, did not have that effect at their time of use. Vocabulary relating to genders and sexualities raises important questions of inclusion and exclusion. When dealing with drag histories, we need to acknowledge that terms that existed and were popular at the time have been reconsidered in the light of contemporary knowledge and understanding today. For example, no longer do we talk about 'transvestites' and 'male/female impersonators' and so on to refer to drag performers, yet these terms were some of the most popular in drag histories. Yet, the use of contemporary labels retrospectively can be seen as anachronistic when we explore the past with the lens and languages of today. It is important to attempt to identify people accurately and respectfully, but, especially in relation to drag, to acknowledge that language shifts throughout time.

Second, there are contextual limitations to our research in this chapter, largely because of the resources available to us. The documentation of history has been a colonial project, and we are aware of the weighting given to drag histories from the Global North in this chapter, given the sources that currently exist. While we do present a number of case studies from Asia, Latin America, and Africa, we eagerly await access to research that enlarges the vision and learning about drag histories from wider linguistic and geographical contexts in the global majority world. In spite of these linguistic and contextual restrictions, the drag histories we offer below illuminate the emergence and survival of a rich art form through years of oppression, stigma and violence.

Third, we are aware that narratives of drag pasts are, in the majority, literally 'his-stories' – stories of men in drag. This cultural bias can still be seen today, and stories of drag kings and non-binary performers remain a minority within a minority. In her research on Sydney's drag king scene, Kerryn Drysdale writes how 'minority social groups can be especially vulnerable if they lack the kind of mainstream attention that guarantees their external existence in formal institutional archives' (2019: 6). Drysdale notes a sense of urgency as a motivation for documenting the stories of the drag kings, as the scene in Sydney would all but disappear within three years. In our survey of histories below, we attempt to redress the balance in our discussion that does not focus exclusively on queens; nonetheless, are aware of these limitations.

HISTORIES/HERSTORIES

The histories/herstories of drag are disparate and fragmented. Drag's past narratives are a collection of stories, told through different lenses with purpose and to distinct audiences. There is no direct access to the past, and therefore all 'evidence' that remains with us are just fragments of larger stories. There is both bias and subjectivity in the telling of such stories, and in accounts of history, there is no exception to this. Most significantly for our purposes, in many areas, the privileged positions of heteronormativity and cisnormativity and their pervading powers have policed what is considered worthy of documentation. Ultimately, much drag practice has simply not been recorded, and many fragments of drag have not seen the light of day. Cultural historians have much work still to do with this, alongside uncovering LGBTQ+ histories/herstories more broadly. Any attempt to make a neat, coherent history of drag, as desirable as that is, would involve an act of editorial violence – whose histories/ herstories do we include? How do we represent what we do not know or that which has not been documented? How do we include voices that now seemed privileged, but were not at their time of writing? How do we continue to pay attention to intersectionality? How do we access research in contexts we are not familiar with, or in languages we do not speak?

As the reader may glean, any attempt to document a concrete, comprehensive starting point of *where* and *when* drag began or to represent historical case studies fully resembles the queer journey to Oz. This involves following a yellow brick road with an uncertain end, signposted with distractions and detours, only to lead to disappointment. Yet, glitter and campness are what makes the journey worthwhile.

Drag research on histories/herstories can be located in one of the most comprehensive collection of essays on the topic of drag history, *Drag Histories, Herstories and Hairstories: Drag in a Changing Scene* (2021). The editors, Edward and Farrier, talk about the task of tracing drag histories/herstories as a 'sequin method' where some sequins (drag stories) shine brighter than others and their stories appear more illuminated. Nonetheless, there are many sequins that make up the whole garment but are often rendered invisible as they fall off or lose their shine. The invisibility, hiddenness or loss of narratives around drag are obviously connected to safety, legal restrictions, homophobia or shame, among other factors. As Edward and Farrier note:

> Queer histories/herstories and hairstories are often unable to be told in the same way as normative histories/herstories. This is mainly because, like many other minority or non-normative lives, LGBTQ+ people have often been rendered invisible, their stories often undocumented, or only recorded in a kind of code, their secrets safely eclipsed by loss and liminality.
>
> (Edward & Farrier 2021: 1)

There will be many drag artists and drag activities that have not been entirely documented throughout time for reasons mentioned here, and unfortunately, we will not be fully aware of their contribution or impact. Overall, drag histories/herstories are complex and messy. Researchers ought to be conscientious and scrutinise for any queer details in cultural landscapes, through both binocular vision and microscopic eyes.

EARLY 'DRAG'

Let us begin with the earliest text we can find. In the Jewish and Christian scriptures, the book of Deuteronomy 22:5 states, 'A woman shall not wear a man's garment, nor shall a man put on a woman's cloak, for whoever does these things is an abomination to the Lord your God'. This 2000+-year-old prohibition has an afterlife beyond its religious context. The law reflects standards in ancient Israelite culture, where clothing signified not only gender but also social status, religious purity, and tribal identity. Martti Nissinen suggests the law was to preserve a distinction between the Israelites and those who worshipped pagan gods. He writes, 'both castration and cross-dressing were signs of devotion to an alien deity, special traits of gender identification and gender roles that were associated with cultures forbidden to the Israelites. Mixing gender roles was not a matter of personal preference or orientation, but a cultural signifier' (Nissinen 1998: 43).

Given the Bible's significant influence on legal codes throughout Western and colonial history, this passage has undoubtedly shaped norms and legislation around gender expression. Its influence lingers even today. In the contemporary United States, for example, this verse has been mobilised by some conservative and religious groups in protests against drag story time, events where drag performers read books to children in libraries. Here, the Bible is used as 'proof' against gender non-conformity, and the lineage from today's anti-drag sentiment can be located in ancient discomforts with gender non-conformity.

Interestingly, the biblical verse condemns women's wearing of men's garments and vice versa; yet, it is historically the male-to-female presentation that has received harder scrutiny and social consequences. Female cross-dressing has been popularised with heroism, at times, such as using disguise to fight as men in wars. For example, Deborah Sampson fought in the American Revolution disguised as a man, and there is the legendary Mulan in Chinese folklore, popularised by the Disney film. Such examples demonstrate how female cross-dressing is seen as noble, brave and patriotic rather than transgressive. In contrast, men adopting feminine attire result in higher criticism and policing, surrounded by discriminatory rhetoric of moral decay, mental illness, or unnatural deviance.

This is entirely linked to patriarchy, misogyny and homophobia. Women and men did not have equal social status in ancient times, and for a man to 'lessen' himself by dressing in attire attributed to women involved a perceived reduction of privilege that raised suspicion and fear. So, while Deuteronomy 22:5 stands as one of the earliest recorded condemnations of what might be called *drag*, its legacy and influence is still potent.

It is worth noting that not all ancient societies shared this anxiety around binary gender roles and rules. In Ancient Egypt (*c.*1479–1458 BCE), Hatshepsut was a female pharaoh, who often is often portrayed as male in art, wearing a false beard and traditional masculine regalia. In ancient Greece, male worshippers in the cult of Dionysus would wear women's clothing. Such ritual cross-dressing formed part of ecstasies. Dionysus is often depicted as androgynous, thereby embodying a disruption of boundaries that was evident in these transgressive ceremonies. Similarly, in many Indigenous North American cultures, Two-Spirit people (a modern, pan-Indigenous term encompassing diverse gender identities beyond the Western male-female binary) are often regarded with deep respect. Rather than being marginalised, they hold important social, sacred roles as healers, ceremonial leaders, matchmakers, name-givers, and keepers of oral traditions. Their ability to embody both masculine and feminine qualities was and is seen not as deviant, but as a gift of spiritual powers. The reverence for Two-Spirit people contrasts sharply with colonial attitudes that imposed rigid gender binaries and suppressed non-conformity to strict gender codes.

'DRAG' IN GREEK AND ROMAN THEATRE

Long before drag's accessories included sequins and stilettos, its tools were masks and sandals. The idea of drag as gender performance reaches back much further than the contemporary stage. In the amphitheatres of ancient Greece and Rome, gender was always already a performance simply because of necessity. In classical theatre, women were barred from acting, so male performers had to take on every role. This sets the stage, figuratively and literally, for drag in performance. Such public performances, where men performed the roles of female characters to narrate the story, highlight a patriarchal culture that excluded women from public visibility and voice. Greek tragedy gives us some of the clearest examples:

Antigone, Electra, Medea would all have been played by men. With the help of masks and stylised movement, 'femininity' was able to be conveyed visually. Masks often featured exaggerated hairstyles or gentle features to signify femininity. These ancient examples revealed how gender has always been constructed. Gender is crafted from codes, not from chromosomes.

Comedy, on the other hand, leaned into the absurd nature of gender as a construct. Aristophanes' plays often used gender as a site of farce. In *Thesmophoriazusae* (411 BCE), the character Euripides is worried that women will retaliate against him for how he portrays them in his plays, so he sends a male relative, Mnesilochus, disguised as a woman to spy on the festival. Mnesilochus's presentation fails, and he is exposed as a man to comedic effect. In similar ways, Roman theatre inherited these conventions and amplified them. Female characters continued to be portrayed by men, with performance often veering into pantomime. Unlike the slapstick we might associate with the modern term 'pantomime', Roman pantomime was a solo, often masked, performance in which a male dancer would play multiple roles, alternating between male and female characters throughout one single performance. These roles were silent, often expressed through dance, gesture, and elaborate costuming, while a chorus narrated the story with musicians. In this example, gender is not represented by bodies or voice, but it is performed by movement, clothing, and mask. In one example from the pantomime myth, *Phaedra and Hippolytus*, a single pantomime performer would play multiple roles, including a grieving queen, a stoic young man, an angry, vengeful father, and a manipulative god. Therefore, recognisability trumped realism in such early representations of 'drag'. These ancient performances remind us that gender on stage has always been crafted, costumed, and codified. In the search for histories/herstories, traces of drag can be found among togas and tragedy.

GENDER AND TRANSFORMATION IN NOH THEATRE (NŌ)

Noh theatre, which emerged in fourteenth-century Japan, is one of the oldest continuous forms of classical performance. Noh is rooted in ritual, poetry and movement and is known for its elegance and symbolic richness. Less concerned with portraying realism, Noh theatre conjures mood through minimalism: a bare wooden stage, a chorus, and haunting tones of flute and drum. A key feature of Noh performance is transformation, as performers shift between characters, emotions, and even worlds (human/spirit). Like other classical traditional Noh is considered an exclusively male-only form (Geilhorn 2017). Men performed female characters, and, in order to do so effectively, masks were essential. When an actor performed a female role, he wore a mask called an *onnamen*. The mask's expression changed depending on a tilt of the head, a movement of the body, and its position under a light. Actors would also transform their voices, altering pitch, tone or rhythm. In Noh, gender is not performed to be questioned or disrupted unlike in drag. Rather, there is a deeper symbolism linked to embodiment; it represents a transformation of becoming something other than oneself. The performance of gender, like everything in Noh, is careful and intentional. Across cultures and histories, the stage has always been a place where identity is constructed and transcended. Indeed, this is the simple purpose of performance and gender performance is no exception.

KABUKI AND THE ART OF GENDER PERFORMANCE

Kabuki theatre developed in Japan in the early seventeenth-century as a world of spectacle. Unlike the restraint of Noh, Kabuki is energetic, characterised through bold costumes, vibrant make-up, dramatic movement, and striking sound. Originally, Kabuki was founded by a woman, Okuni. She was a shrine maiden (*miko*), a role which carries deep cultural and spiritual importance. *Miko* were often thought to have spiritual powers, including the ability to communicate with *kami* (gods or spirits) and enter trance states during rituals. Early Kabuki troupes did include women, and the performances quickly became popular. This was due, in part, to the fact that they blurred the lines between theatre and eroticism. Yet, the government became wary of the perceived indecency of the performance form, and subsequently banned women from performing in 1629. They were replaced by young male performers, who themselves were later banned for similar concerns around morality and decency. Eventually, Kabuki became the domain of adult male actors, and that tradition continues today. This shift gave rise to the *onnagata*: male performers who specialise in female roles. But to call *onnagata* an equivalent of 'female impersonators' would miss the point, as the purpose is not to imitate women; it is about stylised embodiment. Over time, the *onnagata* became a celebrated role in their own right, revered for their beauty. Kabuki theatre is full of transformation: exaggerated representations of the construction of male and female bodies (Gabrovska 2020). In Kabuki, costumes are changed in seconds, voices shift, stages rotate, and, yet again, gender play and performativity is part of this theatrical vocabulary.

ELIZABETHAN (1558–1603) AND JACOBEAN (1603–1625) THEATRE IN ENGLAND

During Elizabethan England (1558–1603) reading and writing became popular, and therefore there is textual evidence about 'drag'. Just like the theatrical forms listed earlier, Elizabethan and Jacobean theatre employed boys and men to perform the roles of girls and women. Women were forbidden from performing on the stage due to social attitudes surrounding principles and decency, and the restriction of women's role in the job market. The practice of women on stage would have been deemed improper, hence the necessity for boys to be *dr*essed *a*s a *g*irl (drag). There are other schools of thought that the term 'drag' evolved from performers 'dragging' the skirts across the floor/boards.

Shakespeare's plays, including *Romeo and Juliet* (*c.*1591–1595) and *Macbeth* (*c.*1603–1607), involved boys whose voices had not yet broken and male actors who trained their vocal cords to achieve a much higher pitched tone. This aimed to transmit a feminine voice. Equally, feminine mannerisms were learnt, rehearsed and then incorporated into the performer's repertoire (Gibson 2000). Various wigs and dresses were worn throughout the plays. These costumes and mannerisms must surely have raised some questions about the role and representation of girls and women, yet they simultaneously prevented any moral push back from the spectators. The prohibition on women performing also allowed boys and men to flourish in the theatre, giving male acting troupes such as Lord Chamberlain's Men or the King's Men opportunities to thrive. However, the rise of Oliver Cromwell (1599–1658), who became Lord Protector of

England, brought about a total ban on theatre. His Puritanical high ground launched a quest to reform England (the period known as The Reformation). He took to banning theatre in 1642 and thereby closing all theatre venues. Cromwell's restrictive outlook associated theatre with sin, especially with the example of men cross-dressing. His cynicism of theatre was grounded in his beliefs that theatre brought with it dishonesty, wickedness, intoxication and, therefore, diverted people from their religious duties in life. Five years after the ban on theatre performances, Cromwell and Parliament passed laws that allowed theatre buildings to be torn down. This 'sin cleansing' resulted in a dismissal of Shakespeare's actors, whose livelihoods and artistry/costumes, were now literally in tatters. Actors had to evolve and seek out new forms of work; some continued to perform but this was underground and risky, done covertly because of the fear of severe punishment.

In the 1660s a brighter future for theatre was on the horizon, as King Charles II lifted the ban. The lifting of the prohibition on theatre brought a revival of theatre spaces. Venues that had been previously closed or demolished were re-opened or rebuilt. New opportunities arose for actors and King Charles's shift in moral direction undid the strict rigidity of Cromwell's Parliament by paving the way, for the first time in England, for women's presence on the stage. Women like Nell Gwynn (the mistress of Charles II) carved out a huge name for themselves in the theatre, along with Anne Bracegirdle. This Restoration period which followed the Reformation period gave women performing opportunities previously denied to them.

During this period, one of the most intriguing figures in gender non-conformity is documented in France. Abbé François-Timoléon de Choisy (1644–1724) was a French courtier and cleric who famously spent time dressing in women's clothing. Raised by a mother who encouraged de Choisy to wear women's clothing from a young age, de Choisy continued this practice into adulthood. De Choisy is one of the most fascinating figures in the history of gender non-conformity, as de Choisy was not known for dressing in feminine attire in the theatre, but in society and everyday life. De Choisy moved through aristocratic circles in dresses and jewels, joining high-society gatherings in full femme presentation. An account of de Choisy's life was published in 1920, entitled *Mémoires de l'Abbé de Choisy habillé en femme* (de Choisy 1920). The book offers a mix of self-reflection and scandal, describing not only the practicalities of dressing 'en femme' but also the pleasure de Choisy took in unsettling social expectations. Whether entirely factual or part self-mythologising, the accounts of de Choisy's life are a rare, early example of someone expressing gender, not as something fixed and fixable, but fluid and fabulous.

MOLLY HOUSES (EIGHTEENTH AND NINETEENTH CENTURIES)

As with most places of subcultural activity, drag had gone under-ground during the Reformation in England. In public, any sus-picion of men dressing in feminine attire or expressing same-sex attraction was firmly policed under watchful eyes. Yet, centuries later, venues of cross-dressing and gender performance had started to take root and thrive in places that had distinctly gender non-conformist vibes; one such example was a molly house. A molly house was the term used for meeting places such as public houses, coffee rooms and private spaces for gay, bisexual and gender non-conforming men during the eighteenth and nineteenth centuries in Britain. These spaces were the embryonic happenings of drag. Evidently, they were in towns and cities with high populations. The houses were a place for mollies to gather and the houses formed part of a gay subculture, giving the mollies a space to play, gossip, be frivolous and meet potential sexual partners.

Prior to the establishment of molly houses, men seeking relation-ships with other men had to ensure activities were private. The term molly was used by gay men to refer to one another. Molly has been written as *molley* and *mollie* and is also linked to the British term *mollycoddled*, meaning 'soft' or 'effeminate'. Linguistically, it is clearly related to the French feminine word *molle* for 'soft'. Culturally the word can be linked to Mary/Moll (a common female name), which later became slang for effeminate men. Historical writer Rictor Norton notes how 'Molly is the word which most gay men used to refer to one another for more than 150 years, a longer period of usage than the quasi-scientific modern term "homosexual"' (Norton 1992: 9). Norton also goes on to explain that 'such terms as "molly" and "gay" are preferable to "homosexual" because they have a greater resonance, and encompass a wider range of ambiguous references which is appropriate to the wider issues of social rather than specifically sexual behaviour' (1992: 9). Indeed, in contemporary usage, the term 'homosexual' often is associated with legal and medical uses, rather than the more popular terms, lesbian, gay or bisexual.

Mollies used to act out relationships as mother and daughter in playful ways, and such relationship dynamics are an antecedent to associations such as 'drag' mothers and families that were popularised through ballroom culture and remain today. Their communication was punctuated with high camp, as they would call each other 'dear' and poke fun at one another. It was through these camp, frivolous and daring interactions that the mollies bonded with one another, away from the constraints of the world. Mollies were also ahead of their time, as they would mock society, and they relished in disrupting gender norms by engaging in bawdy acts of outrageous fun. Such activities played out as mock weddings among the mollies, often lovers who demonstrated a public display of devotion. Similarly, re-enactments of significant ritual events, such as christenings took place, and mollies would enact parodies of giving birth, with others gathering around as midwives. Lively displays of behaviour also included chats with one another using specific words as codes and slang. Norton notes 'gay men within molly subculture developed their own molly slang, called Female Dialect, consisting largely of Maiden Names with which they affectionately christened one another' (Norton 1992: 92). Subsequently, mollies would each be referred to as a *Miss* or *Madam* followed by their given name such as Pomegranate Molly and Garter Mary.

The criminalisation of male 'homosexual' acts rendered male-male sexual activities punishable by imprisonment under the Buggery Act of 1553. Indeed, the punishment also included the death penalty, as male same-sex relations and sexual activities remained a capital offence until 1861. Given the legal situation at the time, frequent raids on the molly houses therefore brought about many arrests and often these raids led to intimidation, threats, and blackmail. One such raid in 1725 was at the house of Margaret Clap (also known as Mother Clap), who, by all accounts, was an exciting and fun seeking cisgender heterosexual woman. Clap ran a coffee house, more than likely her own home, for a period of two years. Speculation on the reasons for Mother Clap's involvement with the mollies are broad:

perhaps she saw economic opportunity, wanted to convey allyship, provide spaces or maybe she simply had a desire to participate in subversion. Her coffee house was situated in Field Lane, Holborn in Middlesex, England. Clap's house served a vibrant community of gender non-conforming and gay and bisexual men; she assisted as the main host offering rooms with beds. She also purchased alcohol for her customers from public houses, for example, at the Bunch o' Grape's tavern (which was next door to her house). The molly house crossed class divides and was a meeting place for men from a range of social backgrounds, including aristocracy. However, in the raid of Clap's coffee house, more than forty mollies had been rounded up, in an invasion which had been steered by the Society for the Reformation of Manners, brought about in 1691. This Reformation focused on vulgarity, sex work and 'sin' as deemed by the society of the time. The men under arrest were taken to prison and awaited trial. Following the raid on Clap's house, more molly houses came under attack from the authorities and subsequently more men were placed in confinement. According to historical records documented in Rictor Norton's *Mother Clap's Molly House: The Gay Subculture in England 1700–1830,* 'most of them were set free due to lack of evidence. A few of them, however, were fined, imprisoned, and exhibited in the pillory, and three men were subsequently hanged at Tyburn' (Norton 1992: 54). These three unfortunate men were named as William Griffin, Gabriel Lawrence, and Thomas Wright. There were uncountable numbers of lives lost through persecution at this time. Often, upon release from prison, those who had been incarcerated died by suicide due to the public humiliation they endured. Others would go on the run in the hope of avoiding shame and further persecution. As Norton (1992) notes, men were often put in the 'pillories', a wooden framework with holes for one's head and hands, in which offenders were exposed to public abuse. It was not unusual for men to die, or come close to death, from being severely beaten while in these pillories. As for Margaret Clap, she was placed in the stocks for public humiliation and sentenced to two years in prison. Her whereabouts thereafter are not recorded.

Edward Ward's *The History of London Clubs* (1709) is a text written during the events of molly culture, and it is openly referred to in the book. Ward does not risk incriminating the mollies or their venue by naming the exact location of the molly house, but he writes about their presence 'at a certain tavern in the city, whose sign I shall not mention because I am unwilling' (Ward 1709: 28). Ward talks briefly about the curious happenings going on behind closed doors. These writings are rare in that the text is written in 1709 and therefore provides a primary source and valuable written account about the mollies through the author's first-hand experience. Yet, despite Ward's protective stance in not naming the venue, his tone is far from flattering. Ward discusses the mollies as being a '[gang] of Wretches in town, who call themselves mollies & are so far degenerated from all Masculine deportment or Manly exercises that they rather fancy themselves women initiating all the little Vanities that Custom has reconcil'd to the female sex, affecting to speak, walk, tattle, curtsy, cry, scold, & mimick all manner of Effeminacy' (Ward 1709: 28). Ward also goes on to discuss the interactions, playful family dynamics, and relationships, as he records 'every one was to talk of their Husbands & Children, one Estolling the virtues of her Husband, another the genius and wit of their Children; whilst a Third would express himself sorrowfully under the character of a Widow' (Ward 1709: 28). These accounts would have certainly had tongues wagging about the mollies' scandalous and unusual behaviour. At the same time, it would also ignite recognition in the consciousness of the curious, who could feel validated by others' existence, as it gives visibility to same-sex desire and gender non-conformity. Such knowledge would have been undoubtedly priceless at a time when individuals had to restrain their gender non-conformity or same-sex desires.

'THERE IS NOTHING LIKE A DAME': PANTOMIME PERFORMANCE

British pantomime has long provided a theatrical home for drag performance, even though it has not been named as 'drag' specifically. Widely accepted as part of festive traditions, the pantomime (or 'panto' as it is often abbreviated) is familiar to British audiences as a staple of Christmas events. In these theatre performances, mainly targeted at family audiences, the pantomime dame is a parodic, hyper-feminised character played by a man in bold, extravagant and often cartoon type costumes.

The origins of the pantomime dame were heavily influenced by the *commedia dell'arte* characters of the early modern European stage. *Commedia dell'arte* was a form of sixteenth-century Italian improvisational theatre featuring stock characters, physical comedy, and masks. It made its evolution to pantomime through British *harlequinade* traditions. *Harlequinade* was a comic theatrical genre that evolved in eighteenth-century Britain, centring on the mischievous character Harlequin and performed as a slapstick-filled interlude or afterpiece to a performance. Eventually it became a key part of early pantomime. In the nineteenth century, through the popular form of the music hall, the pantomime dame was popularised. One of the most influential figures in this development was Dan Leno, who became a household name as a principal boy and later as a dame at the Theatre Royal, Drury Lane (Radcliffe 2011). Leno's performances were shaped by a finely honed physical comedy, absurd costumes, and the rhythms of working-class speech. His portrayal of characters such as Mother Goose or Widow Twankey relied on excessive exaggeration, thereby positioning the dame as something entirely constructed and joyfully artificial. Through the characters, the figure of the dame often served to parody social expectations of womanhood, poking fun at domestic roles, poverty, and authority.

The dame has always been a performance of excess: oversized breasts, padding, impossible wigs, and deliberately grotesque makeup. But the dame's performance is safely contained; her drag is always humorous or slapstick. Crucially therefore, the pantomime dame is an acceptable form of drag and queerness, as she is far removed from contemporary issues relating to gender and sexual politics, even when articulating some adult-orientated innuendos that go over the heads of young children. There is a naivety to the dame character that dilutes any sort of political or activist potential. Yet, the dame presents us with a curious cultural contradiction. At a time when drag queens reading to children in libraries provokes moral panic in some parts of the USA, in the UK the pantomime dame (essentially a drag performer by any other name) has an unquestionable central role in this form of family entertainment. The contradiction reveals the ways in which gender performance is policed, not by what it is, but by who performs it and where. In this way, there is a cultural compartmentalisation when we compare pantomime drag to drag queen story hour events. Here, the moral panic is around children's 'exposure' to drag, where drag is reframed as dangerous, inappropriate, or corrupting. And yet, similar age children are taken by schools to pantomimes where they laugh at a man in an oversized dress making jokes about his multicoloured bloomers. Pantomime dames are seemingly protected by codewords such as 'tradition' and 'nostalgia'. Still, drag queens reading to children are vulnerable to politicised scrutiny precisely because their function is to represent education around issues of diversity and inclusion.

The pantomime dame reminds us that drag has long been part of Britain's theatrical traditions. While the dame became a fixture of festive theatre, her presence also laid the groundwork for drag's migration into music halls, as is later discussed. By the mid-nineteenth century, as music hall emerged as a dominant form of working-class entertainment, the familiarity of drag as comic device was already embedded in the cultural imagination.

While much early drag history is mapped through European examples such as the molly houses and music halls, it is crucial to remember that acts of drag performance and resistance were also emerging in subcultural spaces. In late-nineteenth-century America, William Dorsey Swann (1860–1923), a Black former enslaved person, organised 'drag balls' in Washington, DC, laying claim to drag spaces. Swann embodied drag as political defiance. Arrested multiple times for 'impersonating a woman', Swann boldly petitioned for a presidential pardon, the first known American to do so in defence of LGBTQ+ assembly rights. This request was denied. Importantly, Swann referred to himself as the 'queen of drag', marking one of the first recorded uses of the term 'queen' in relation to non-conforming drag identity and performance.

DRAG AND BLACKFACE

The history of drag has some uncomfortable and problematic roots, some that persist to this day (see Chapter 2). One such relationship that emerges in drag history is its interface with blackface minstrelsy, a combination that actually served to popularise the form. Blackface emerged in the United States in the 1820s and 1830s. The minstrel shows were popular, where white performers darkened their skin with burnt cork to caricature Black people. These performances were heavily built on dehumanising stereotypes, yet they were a popular feature in American entertainment. At the same time, they helped to influence the popularity of drag in performance, due to their emphasis on exaggerated identity, costume, and character work.

Minstrels actually first began appearing in whiteface with fair wigs, known as the Albino Family. They swapped to blackface and were later known as the Harmoneons. Marhsall S. Pike (1818–1901) was the first female minstrel. Edwin P. Christy formed Christy's Minstrels and his stepson, George N. Christy, emerged as a leading blackface performer during the early years of minstrel shows in the 1840s. They performed *Lucy Long*, a song that had tones of feminine seduction and stolen glances.

There are multiple representations of drag in the form. Anthony Slide comments that 'the first female impersonators were heavy-built characters for whom dresses were nothing more than stage contrivances' (1986: 16–17). Characters such as Leon (or 'The Only Leon') had an extensive wardrobe of refined dresses, gowns, accessories and a soprano voice. In 1870, the New York Clipper described Leon as 'the best male female actor known to the stage' (cited in Slide 1986: 16). In many minstrel productions, performers such as Thomas Dilverd would use blackface and drag, often simultaneously. Some performers were known simply by one name 'Bernardo' (Thomas White) or Ricardo (Foley McKeever).

The figure of the 'mammy' was wholly problematic. It was often performed by a white man in both blackface and drag, thereby reinforcing intersecting racist and sexist tropes: an early form of *misogynoir* (anti-Black racism towards women). This mocked and marginalised both Black people and women; it was simultaneously racist and misogynist. Black performers like Bert Williams (1874–1922), himself forced to wear blackface despite being Black, navigated these constraints with great difficulty. For Black drag artists particularly, the requirement to conform to damaging racial stereotypes exposes how embedded racism was in theatres and other cultural spaces. Black performers, such as Williams, had to endure systemic racist practices in order to have a career in the entertainment industry.

Contemporary drag continues to wrestle with uncomfortable histories such as this. While the modern drag scene has largely distanced itself from blackface, issues of cultural appropriation and racist systems of exclusion remain (see Chapters 2 and 3). By the early twentieth century, the minstrel show was replaced by vaudeville and variety theatre.

THE POPULARITY OF MUSIC HALL

Progressive attitudes had generated a shift from men playing women's stage roles in the Elizabethan era, to women playing men's stage roles in the nineteenth century. In the 1850s, during the reign of Queen Victoria in England, music halls had started to take root and later became part of the fabric of British culture. In the early days of music hall, the venues were often extensions of bars or pubs; they were loud, lively spaces where the draw for the public was primary the consumption of alcohol, and performances were secondary to drinking. These were often working-class venues, and the entertainment served as a backdrop to drinking and socialising. As time moved on, the halls became more legitimate places of entertainment in their own right, attracting mass audiences.

Early twentieth-century female impersonator Malcolm Scott (1872–1929) had a significant role to play in the visibility and reputation of drag in music halls. Scott 'was a trailblazer not only as a female impersonator, but as a satirical comedian on the music hall stage in the Edwardian era' (Sculthorpe 2022: xiv). Scott delighted both UK and American audiences with his unique style of parodying famous contemporary and historical women, such as Queen Elizabeth I and Cleopatra. Scott often went under the banner of 'The Woman Who Knows', a know-it-all socialite who gave commentaries on etiquette and fashion. One of Scott's contemporaries, Bert Errol (1883–1949), also gained a reputation for himself as a female impersonator. Errol's stage shows used extravagant gowns and he sang in a high-pitched tone. Errol successfully toured many countries such as South Africa, Canada and the USA (Bloomfield 2023). Barbette (1899–1973), too, had a vibrant stage presence and successful career in drag and as an aerial performer. As an acrobatic aerialist, Barbette would perform trapeze and tightrope routines in full drag. At the end of the act, Barbette would sometimes dramatically reveal himself as male, shocking audiences who had assumed they were watching a woman the entire time.

These early-twentieth-century drag performers epitomised glamour and style; as Bloomfield notes:

> in addition to the dame, a newer style of female impersonation was resonating with British theatregoers by the 1870s. This type of female impersonation, which would eventually be referred to as glamour drag, featured stylish, elegant, and deliberately alluring renderings of femininity that often drew from images of contemporary female stars.
>
> (Bloomfield 2023: 21)

Similarly, vaudeville had evolved from France. Vaudeville is thought to originate from 'voix de ville' (voice of the town), and its *divertissement* made its way to French speaking Canada and then North America. Vaudeville mirrored the style of music hall with renowned songs, acts, performers, and dances. Ballet was especially popular as a segment. Unlike music hall, where ballet dancers were not respected, vaudeville had a higher appreciation of the form. Also, during the early twentieth century the American female impersonator Julian Eltinge (1881–1941) had garnered a reputation for himself as a talented 'drag' performer. Eltinge captivated audiences with beauty and stylish dresses; he not only toured theatres but also starred in silent films such as *The Fascinating Widow* (1913), where he played both male and female roles. Eltinge was one of the earliest drag artists to achieve cinematic fame. In fact, so successful was Eltinge that the Eltinge Theatre in New York was named after him (1913), later becoming the Empire Theatre on 42nd Street. However, towards the roaring 1920s, music hall (and later vaudeville) started to fade into the theatre wings with the advent of variety entertainment.

Variety performance transcended onto the radio waves and then onto television screen (see Chapter 3). If we flick through the many history books and watch the plethora of documentaries on Victorian England, we can clearly see how this period had been deemed conservative, puritanical and prudish: hefty garments, emphasis on restraint, appearances of nobility, and censoring of the body in public. Male same-sex relationships remained illegal. In theatres, previous plays were revised and purified for morality purposes. This was also an era where opposition to such norms countered strict social expectations and regulations. If we take a sneaky peek into some of the goings on during Victoria's time on the throne while she was known for saying 'we are not amused', it is obvious that people were amused during the Victorian period. Some delighted in pornography and sex work was widespread, as Richard Anthony Baker in his text *British Music Hall: An Illustrated History* notes:

> Victorian England does not deserve its reputation for prudery. The idea that the nineteenth century middle class was so offended by nakedness that piano legs were covered up is a ludicrous legend. The truth, albeit concealed, was that pornography was rife, as was prostitution, especially child prostitution. More than 50,000 prostitutes operated in London in the middle of the century.
>
> (Baker 2022: 1)

Among the many deviant acts and nocturnal adventures during this time, the trial of Oscar Wilde represents one of the earliest publicly documented uses of the term 'queer' in a derogatory, sexuality-related context. In 1895 the Marquis of Queensberry had referred to Wilde as a 'snob queer' in his letter expressing his repulsion towards Wilde and his own son Lord Alfred Douglas (National Archives 2021). Legal enforcements ran parallel to a cultural rise in popularity of drag and 'queer' performance in music halls and vaudeville theatres.

'KINGS' OF MUSIC HALL

During this era, male impersonators were visible on the stages of music halls and vaudeville theatres, and their presence challenged gender expectations and public ideas of masculinity. Early male impersonation had a real intelligence to the form, as the performers held a mirror up to masculinity. Such performances drew audiences and packed out theatres. They laid down the early foundations for what we now understand as drag kinging, even though that term would not emerge until decades later in the late 1980s and 1990s. These drag pioneers speak back to a drag culture saturated in queens, as Stephen Farrier writes 'we live in a patriarchy, therefore much is written and said about drag queens and their history but less so about kings. It is important to deal with this imbalance and come to understand, in particular, how drag kings' relationships to audiences contributes to the history of the form overall' (2021: 57).

Annie Hindle (*c*.1840–1897) was one of the earliest known male impersonators in the USA, and was already well-established by the late nineteenth century. Hindle had an ability to mimic male gestures, vocal tones, and working-class swagger. Controversy followed when Hindle married a woman while dressed in male clothing, thereby further complicating gender norms. Similarly, Ella Wesner (1841–1917) played the part of the dandy to perfection, dressed in tailored suits, top hats, and tuxedos. Wesner's niece, Maggie Western, followed in this tradition, but with less popularity. Other contemporaries include Zelma Rawlston (born Zelma Stuchenholz), Florence Tempest (born Claire Lilian Ijames), and Kitty Doner (born Catherine Donohoe), who took to stages with sharp acts and parodied masculinity through exaggeration and intricate theatrical timing.

Black performers took part in male impersonation and reshaped it. The performances of Florence Hines (1868–1924) and Bert Whitman (*c*.1887–1964) added cultural weight to the impersonation of the dandy, given the racial politics of the time. Gladys Bentley (1907–1960) was big in voice, body, and presence. Known also as Bobbie Minto and Fatso Bentley, she stomped across Harlem Renaissance stages in full tuxedo, belting out blues songs at the piano. With her success, Bentley made no secret of her lesbian identity, which in turn brought both admiration and intense scrutiny. This was during a time when such openness was virtually unheard of, especially for a Black, gender non-conforming performer. As one of the highest paid Black performers in the USA, Bentley's success can be seen as a triumph in spite of the brutal realities of racism in entertainment and society. Collaboratively, these artists paved the way for contemporary drag kinging.

Examples of gender impersonation can also be found in entertainment in Argentina. Azucena Maizani (1903–1970), known as 'La Ñata Gaucha' stood out in the country's tango scene for her deliberate use of male-coded clothing and rural gaucho imagery. Maizani chose to dress and perform like a tango-singing man in a radical subversion of machismo. In Argentina, the leading role in tango was traditionally reserved for hyper-masculine men. The gaucho was a national symbol of rugged masculinity in Argentina, and therefore, her nickname, *La Ñata Gaucha* means 'the snub-nosed gaucho girl'. Her title, like her performance, was gender-charged.

In England, Matilda Alice Powles (1864–1952), known widely as Vesta Tilley, and Winifred Emms (1883–1972), known as Hetty King, became household names. Tilley's act was razor-sharp comedy; she parodied the upper-class dandy, with top hat, monocle and all. Tilley and King entertained and poked fun politically at the leisurely looseness and perceived laziness of the aristocracy. Tilley's mockery of the gentrified was a huge hit with the working-class masses. She captivated these audiences with an original brand of gender and class subversion by sending up the dandy and toff. Just as Gladys Bentley had received much admiration, Tilley also received much fan mail, especially from women, but she was careful to avoid any hint of scandal. On this matter, Doonan writes, 'Tilley worked hard to vanquish any hint of vice or sleaze from her public image. She made a point of wearing sumptuous high-fashion frocks off-stage, thereby maintaining an image of heterosexual opulence and respectability' (Doonan 2019: 79). Farrier also notes that 'there is evidence that watching Hetty King or Vesta Tilley's acts awakened, reinforced or simply turned on desires for some women. Women wrote desirous love/fan letters' (Farrier 2021: 63).

One of Tilley's more notable acts was *Burlington Bertie*, dating back to 1900. Tilley's costume was a direct swipe at the attire worn by the aristocracy and her swagger across the stage satirised the idle posturing of the upper classes. This act became so popular that it was replicated in the USA, where Tilley's *Burlington Bertie* would be playfully mocked by Ella Shields (1879–1952), a male impersonator from Baltimore. Adapting Tilley's classic *Burlington Bertie* act into *Burlington Bertie from Bow*, Shields's husband had re-worded the song and added '*from Bow*' to the title. Shields would humorously perform and sing this while making a nod towards the audience of the send-up of Tilley. There are layers of complexity to this parody; as well as mocking masculine representation and class, Shields was a performer parodying another performer who parodied masculinity!

Hetty King (1883–1972), like Tilley, was based in England and originally from the northwest. At the start of her career, she had started out as a performer under the guidance of her father, Billy King, and toured in his company. She played out male parts in pantomime and eventually sailed overseas to the USA, taking her brand of male impersonation, signature acts and songs with her. King's more notable song 'Ship Ahoy! (All the Nice Girls Love a Sailor)' (1908) brought her much success and recognition. King dressed in aristocratic ways, donning a three-piece suit with matching hat – a costume suitable for playing the gentrified gentleman.

THE PANSIES

In 1920s and 1930s, flamboyant male entertainers known as the pansies became very popular. With their painted faces and feathered gestures, they sparkled across vaudeville and early nightclub circuits. The so-called 'pansy craze' was a full-blown fad in subculture clubs that were underground in New York. Audiences were thrilled to see pansy performers like Karyl Norman (1897–1947) (*The Creole Fashion Plate*) and Ray Bourbon (1892–1971), who sang sentimental songs that were punctuated with sarcasm. Clubs like Harlem's Ubangi Club booked drag as cabaret. The pansy scene balanced a tightrope; they played queer enough to titillate, but sought to keep it coded for respectability. By the early 1930s, a swing to conservatism pushed the pansies out; some were jailed, others escaped and disappeared.

A true star of the early drag circuit, Gene Malin (1908–1933) was openly gay (rare then, rarer still in showbiz) and did not bother with 'female impersonation' as illusion. Malin was not 'full' drag; he was a flamboyant, camp, openly gay male wearing a tuxedo. Malin headlined Manhattan's Club Abbey and outperformed top billing acts through his sheer wit and artistry. He sang, bantered, insulted, teased, and held court all as an emcee. It is important to remember that this was a decade of crackdowns, and here Malin stood defiantly visible until his tragic death in 1933, thrown from a car after a nightclub gig in Los Angeles.

FROM WAR TO WARDROBES

Although male impersonation had packed out music halls and variety shows, by the early twentieth century their popularity was waning. Audience preferences seemed to shift from theatre spaces into clubs, café bars, and, eventually war zones. World War I (1914–1918) upended every form of entertainment. As countries from across the globe were pulled into the trenches, drag followed, functioning as a form of entertainment, escapism, and a booster of morale. In improvised soldier revues and cabaret bunkers, performers dragged up for the troops. As this was a period of restriction and rationing, gowns were borrowed, and make-up and lipstick were smuggled. Drag became a source of laughter and spirit-lifting. In the inter-war period, Splinters were a group of drag performers from the armed forces from World War I, who then toured around Britain with their show. Kirk and Heath note how Splinters 'had capacity audiences in large venues, made three films and was still entertaining concert parties in the late thirties' (Kirk & Heath 1984: 16).

After World War I in Germany, the Weimar Republic (1918–1933) saw Berlin's explosion of queer nightlife. Bars like Eldorado were celebrated for drag. Men wore satin, women wore trousers, and trans performers and drag queens all found stage space. The cabaret scene was bold, bawdy, and increasingly politicised. These forms of cross-dressing entertainment were popular among the working classes to the upper ranks of Nazi officers like Ernst Röhm, who reportedly frequented Eldorado before the purges began.

Parallel to this backdrop of queer nightlife, Magnus Hirschfeld (1869–1935) and his Institute for Sexual Science were building a scientific, social, and political framework for understanding gender variance in Berlin. Through pioneering work and interventions, trans and gender non-conforming people were offered support, visibility and medical transition options. It was the first formal space of its kind, and a sanctuary for many. Inevitably, when Hitler rose to power in 1933, Berlin's nightlife was shut down and Hirschfeld's archive was looted and burned. Bars like Eldorado were raided and closed. The same officers who once applauded drag acts in shows now muscled in and outlawed them. Drag went underground, as many performers fled, disguised themselves, or vanished. In this new regime, to cross dress could mean a prison sentence; to be visibly queer could mean death.

Yet, for allied troops, the Entertainments National Service Association (ENSA) produced shows featuring male soldiers in skirts. Wartime drag was necessarily dressed as frivolity in times when entertainment was limited. Its influence remained in the decades that followed. Drag scholar Jacob Bloomfield examines ex-servicemen's relationship with drag in 'Soldiers in Skirts: Cross-Dressing Ex-Servicemen, Sexuality and Censorship in Post-War

Britain' (2021). Bloomfield's work highlights the importance of the drag troupe 'Soldiers in Skirts', an all-male drag review show, which helped to shape drag's place in a society during a time when moral codes on how masculinity and femininity were heavily regulated. For most part the ex-servicemen were well received, however, Bloomfield's research also delves into the historical records and the complaints received by the Lord Chamberlain's office. Such complaints were centred on the perceived immorality of ex-soldiers in skirts and public disapproval. Overall, ex-servicemen in drag formed part of the British variety entertainment industry, leaving a historical legacy that is not widely known.

Post-World War II bars offered drag shows with a mix of cabaret, burlesque and vaudeville, possibly due to the popularity with soldiers during the war. Drag resurfaced and took a breath in new spaces, as audience appreciation revitalised an art form once 'at risk'. Queer underground venues gave drag a rise in presence and growth. Drag performers took to the stage alongside risqué striptease acts, especially the 'fan dance' which was a favourite among crowds. The Garden of Allah opened in 1946, and was based in Seattle. It operated 'underground' via a hotel basement: 'The Garden of Allah cabaret was the city's first gay-owned gay bar and one of the first in the country' (Paulson & Simpson 1996: xii). Legendary artists like Jackie Starr (1912–1986) and Skippy LaRue (1921–2003) could be seen in glamour drag. The place attracted a varied range of audiences. According to Paulson and Simpson, audiences included a 'mixture of gays, lesbians, tourists, and servicemen', who 'gave way to edgy crowds of blacks and whites, young people fired up by blues and impatient with mellow ballads' (Paulson & Simpson 1996: xi). During the performances of female impersonations, the bar was seldom stormed by the gangsters who wanted to monopolise the venue. The space was 'protected' by the local police who were known for taking bribes and backhanders from the proprietors. This ensured drag, normally heavily discriminated against, was able to perform in safer settings.

1960S–1990S

While theatres had gilt pillars and cabaret venues had red velvet curtains, in contrast, pubs offered cigarette haze and beer-stained stages. Yet, this trade-off of glamour for grit proved generative for drag and for LGBTQ+ visibility. From the 1950s onwards, the pub stage has been drag's laboratory: a place to test material against an audience close enough to spot the imperfect make-up and beads of sweat, quick to heckle and quicker to cheer.

In London's Soho district, Danny La Rue (1927–2009) had achieved success throughout the 1950s, and later opened his night-club, Danny La Rue's, in 1964, which attracted celebrities and royalty (and gangsters such as the Kray twins). Here Princess Margaret could be seen enjoying herself in all her finery, and, on one occasion, Judy Garland and Liza Minnelli could be heard singing impromptu songs with drag stars. The club was a hot bed of high society with La Rue holding attention through back-to-back cabaret songs and comedic acts. It was a judicious mix of comedy sketches juxtaposed with glamourous performances, played out with feathers, sequins, diamante jewels, and lots of champagne (see Chapter 3).

Meanwhile, on the other end of the drag glamour gamut was Mrs Gladys Shufflewick, created by Rex Jameson (1924–1983), who had previously trodden the boards of variety theatre. Jameson had been made TV personality of the year during the 1950s, and had played to many family audiences. He had also been a regular feature on radio, starting out on the BBC's *Variety Bandbox*. Shufflewick's career moved into working-men's pubs with a stand-up comedy show as a Cockney char lady (an old-fashioned term for a cleaner). Shufflewick had an aesthetic that was the total opposite of the likes of Danny La Rue and a complete visual contrast to many of the up-and-coming drag performers. Shufflewick often wore plastic look-ing neck beads and hats with flowers shooting out of them, seeking to characterise the look of a matured char lady on an afternoon out. Her act and look was a deliberate construction and resembled a smash and grab in the local charity/thrift shop. To match her look, her tongue could be salacious and it would make the most risqué of people blush. However, Mrs Shufflewick was able to adapt the act according to the audience. Later in her career, Shufflewick moved from theatre into London pubs like the Black Cap and the Royal Vauxhall Tavern (RVT), this was in part due to theatre clo-sures. Patrick Newley's *The Amazing Mrs Shufflewick: The Life and Times of Rex Jameson* discusses how Shufflewick was '"discovered" by gay audiences in London clubs and pubs and went on to become a cult figure' (2007: 11), thanks to a rise in popularity among the

LGBTQ+ community. The Royal Vauxhall Tavern and Elephant and Castle pubs also gave rise to drag performer Regina Fong (Reg Bundy, 1946–2003), who was part of the sophisticated comedy trio drag act in the late 1970s The Disappointer Sisters. Fong had a residency as a drag compère in the 1980s. Fong mashed up songs in her own branded way, and lip-synced with an intelligence and wit that commanded the attention of the audiences.

As the 1960s opened, British law still classed male same-sex intimacy as a criminal offence (Sexual Offences Act 1956). Yet every Saturday night in South London, drag performers gained momentum. Drag's shift from cabaret to public bars should be read in the zeitgeist of youth rebellion and liberation. British Teddy Boys swaggered into the 1960s in drape coats and quiffs, rejecting post-war conformity; mods had amphetamines and Italian scooters; hippies flooded London and the USA with LSD and paisley textiles. Each subculture made its own contribution to subverting gender politics.

In West Germany, American GIs spent Deutsch Marks on Kölsch and camp at Cologne's Chez Nous. Earlier, Berlin's fabled Eldorado had showcased drag until the Nazis padlocked its doors in 1933; yet three decades later the same street hosted the Crazed Horse Saloon, proof that camp can out-weigh jackboots. Drag at Chez Nous and Berlin's SchwuZ venue mixed parody, political bite, and glamorous drag performances. Chez Nous in Berlin outlasted many of its contemporaries. Operating from 1960 through 2007, it was a popular cabaret bar and refuge for LGBTQ+ community. Surviving both the Cold War and reunification, Chez Nous became drag's embassy in Berlin.

Names mattered, too: the drag queen Coccinelle (1931–2006) headlined at Paris's famous Le Carrousel, allegedly charging more per set than Edith Piaf did just a few streets away. Just a cobblestone away from the tourist throng of the Quartier Pigalle in Paris, Madame Arthur's pulsed with chanson and chicness. Revived in the 1950s and later fused with another show theatre, Le Divan du Monde, it offered a lineup where glamour queens lip-synced to Edith Piaf in feathers, while drag kings delivered Brecht in braces. Paris's Le Monocle, once a women-only bohemian bar, reopened its basement to serve drag kings in tuxedos and patrons in sailor gear. These resurrections of drag in post-war contexts mattered. They stitched a thread of continuity through threat and rupture, surviving oppressive regimes to keep bright lights burning.

Across the Atlantic, San Francisco's Finocchio's and New York's 82 Club flouted liquor-board restrictions. They designated queens as 'female impersonators' and their audiences as 'tourists', a semantic subtlety that kept police raids at bay, unlike at Stonewall (see Chapter 2 for details on Stonewall). Seattle's Garden of Allah revived its pre-war reputation for cabaret. The Jewel Box Revue, America's first racially integrated drag show, ran coast to coast in the 1950s and 1960s with a playbill boasting '25 men and one real girl'. Stormé was the lone drag king among glamour queens. Stormé DeLarverie (1920–2014), the drag king often credited with throwing the first punch at Stonewall, toured the Jewel Box Revue alongside René Del Rio and Baby Martell. The French Box Revue glittered with rhinestones on both coasts, and Powder Puff Revue snuck drag into Las Vegas revues. This rise in drag performance spaces meant drag was commercially viable and desirable.

By June 1967 the 'Summer of Love' had spread west-coast psychedelia across jukeboxes and, by the decade's close, pub drag had carved an awkward truce with the law. British partial decriminalisation of homosexuality in 1967 did not end police harassment, but it emboldened landlords. Similarly, the consequences of the Stonewall Riots kept police from persecuting patrons and venues. Venues like the Crazed Horse Saloon in Paris showcased high-end burlesque and was visited by celebrities.

In the 1970s, drag performers took to stages in ways that were more political, more public, and often more punk. In the shadows of Stonewall, protest was part of the act. In New York, queens lip-synced speeches from the Gay Liberation Front before launching into Shirley Bassey. At Toronto's Club Manatee and Boston's Other Side, drag shared space with activism, erotica, and performance art: a Venn diagram scrawled in eyeliner on the back of a cigarette packet. The 1970s also complicated drag's edges. Performers like International Chrysis (1951–1990) and Jayne County (1947–; from Wayne County and the Electric Chairs) blurred the lines between drag, transition, and stage persona.

Disco culture borrowed heavily from drag, too. Clubs like Paradise Garage in New York and Heaven in London throbbed with sequins and sweat to disco and high energy music. Harlem's ballroom scene began to coalesce in this decade, laying the foundations (literally and metaphorically) for drag houses and chosen family networks.

Crystal LaBeija (1930–1982), outraged by racism in the pageant scene, founded the House of LaBeija and launched the format for underground drag balls. Ballrooms were battlegrounds of camaraderie and competition, with categories like 'executive realness' and 'butch queen vogue femme'. Here, runway walking was an act of resistance, survival and solidarity.

British mainstream pubs started to include drag as part of afternoon and evening entertainment. Pubs embraced drag into their weekly shows, billing the likes of Bunny Lewis (1937–2008). Lewis was based in Manchester and toured the working men's pubs and clubs with a busty blonde aesthetic. Lewis sang live and can be seen in the 1972 film *A Couple of Beauties* and the 1968 drag documentary *What's a Girl Like You …* (see Chapter 3). Another drag legend based in Manchester was Frank 'Foo Foo' Lammar (1937–2003); Lammar owned his own club, named Foo Foo's Palace, which opened in the city of Manchester in 1975. This spot attracted a diverse clientele, mainly heterosexual women. Often coach parties of women arrived on hen nights and sought to be entertained by Foo Foo's own brand of cabaret and individual style of songs.

Between the 1960s until the late 1970s the glossy magazines *Female Mimics International* (also known as *FMI*) and *Guys in Drag* and *Drag Magazine* formed part of a subcultural literature that explored the world of 'female impersonation'. Undoubtedly, these publications were aimed at performers, or, to use the terms popular at the time, 'cross-dressers' and 'transvestites'. Tucked inside its pages were tips, photos, and narrative stories of gender rebellion. These glossy publications claimed to be about promoting glamour, yet a number of the photoshoots portrayed are clearly fetishist and sexualised. The magazines do give in-depth interviews with 'female impersonators', offering a window into the rare histories/herstories of drag performance that are only documented in this form before mass video recording became popular. The artists discuss their drag acts and the night clubs that hosted them, providing tips on wig styling, and choosing accessories and clothing. The magazine was also an early glimpse into drag as consumerist culture, as classified advertisements at the back of the magazines reveal markets for fetish products and even drag consultancy courses. One such place that sold apparel specifically was Uba's Fashions (a boutique located in Venice, California). Here, 'female impersonators' and 'transvestites' would be able to purchase garments, without suspicious policing eyes from shop staff. In later years, *FMI* came under much criticism from drag artists, specifically in letters in the readers' write-in columns, for its sexualisation and sexual objectification of female impersonation with its soft porn imagery and sex ads, betraying its veneer and purpose as a magazine journaling the artistry of drag performance work.

The 1980s were characterised by HIV, high hair, and hard lessons, as AIDS entered the bars like a silent bouncer. At this time, obituaries outnumbered bookings, yet pubs became triage centres for grief fundraising and action. The 1980s saw a shift in how drag was being seen. This was the era of popularity for traditional (trad) drag, with its sequins, feather boas and big wigs. Drag was being revamped with a new energy and more edgy aesthetics thanks to fun pub culture (Brady 2024). Out were the old songs and acts and in came the new with the likes of Dave Dale, who would often parody leather men and lumberjack queens, poking fun at plastic masculinity among his drag repertoire (Oremland 1984). The drag ensemble LSD formed part of these pub acts in the 1980s; the abbreviation stood for Lily, Sandra, and David (Lily Savage, Sandra Hush, and David Dale). This trio of drag helped to shape a booming industry of drag and pub life in London. LSD performed comedy sketches, parodies taken from popular culture laced with acerbic humour and camp. At the same time, comedian Julian Clary with his 'Joan Collins Fan Club' (and Fanny the Wonder Dog) was now taking to the stage and screen wearing queer gothic/PVC attire, which would cement camp and queer's popularity. Alternative (alt) drag was forming its own momentum away from the Shirley Bassey and Judy Garland songs, a mixture of punk and gender rebellion.

Diane Torr launched 'Man for a Day' workshops in the early 1990s in Glasgow; yet they later toured internationally to cities such as Oslo, Zagreb, and Melbourne. The workshops represent a significant intervention in drag practice for two reasons: (1) a focus on the critical parody of masculinities; and (2) a movement from stage performance to social interactions. Distinct from stage-based drag kinging, Torr's workshops were sociological experiments in gender performativity among public participants, who were mostly women. Torr guided the participants through the embodied behaviours, gestures, and social cues typically associated with normative masculinity (First

Hand Films 2014). The aim was experimental gender play: to try on masculinity in public spaces and reflect on the power structures embedded in everyday gender performativity and privilege. Torr's drag-sociology became a form of embodied critique.

RuPaul's *Supermodel (You Better Work)* cracked MTV in 1993, but the runway polish seen on screen was forged by RuPaul in bars like Atlanta's Weekends and Detroit's Menjo's. Pub/bar drag fed mainstream drag, not the reverse. In Britain, Lily Savage leapt from the Elephant & Castle's Royal Vauxhall stage to TV on Channel 4's morning television programme, *The Big Breakfast*. Drag's popularity in the 1990s was not confined to the Global North, and two interesting case studies of drag thriving in South Africa and India are worthy of detailed discussion below.

DRAG PERFORMANCE IN SOUTH AFRICA IN THE 1990S

In South Africa, drag played a surprisingly prominent role as the country transitioned out of apartheid in the early 1990s. A drag character named Evita Bezuidenhout became a nationwide sensation. Bezuidenhout is the creation of performer Pieter-Dirk Uys (1945–), who donned a wig, heels, and an Afrikaans-accented persona to play an outspoken white ambassador's wife. Bezuidenhout delivered biting social comedy about apartheid's social restrictions and class. Remarkably, Bezuidenhout was not only popular in cabarets for parody, but she became politically influential. She took part in voter education campaigns leading up to the 1994 democratic elections and even famously 'interviewed' President Nelson Mandela on television. In November 1994, Mandela sat down with Bezuidenhout for a televised chat, and this was a symbol of how far the country had come; a once-banned performer in drag was now literally at the side of the president, using humour to bridge old divides (Hills 2013). Mandela was a fan of this satirical drag, as he recognised that humour could unite. By embodying an Afrikaner matriarch who has to adapt to the new Rainbow Nation (often bumbling comically in the process), the drag character Bezuidenhout offered critical perspectives on the cultural politics of South Africa. This is a powerful example of drag performance culture contributing to social commentary and change.

Beyond the political stage, South Africa in the 1990s had a vibrant drag pageant scene. In Cape Town and Johannesburg, drag pageants had been running for years (particularly in communities of the Western Cape, where drag pageantry has long been part of holiday carnival traditions). By the 1990s these pageants and club revues were drawing loyal crowds. Legendary performers like Dainti Delischia, the creation of Charles Whiley (1937–2015), reigned as 'mother' of the scene. Delischia was known for her huge wig and quick wit, and first started performing in the 1980s. By the 1990s she was a staple at gay clubs and Pride events, earning the nickname 'the mother of South African drag' (De Barros 2015). Drag queens in South Africa still faced social stigma (homosexuality was only fully decriminalised in 1998), but LGBTQ+ communities found strength in gathering at venues in Cape Town and Johannesburg. These shows were often cabaret with comedy skits and lip-sync performances of diva ballads. It was also common to see a queen don a feathered headdress and perform as local music icons, such as Brenda Fassie or Mariam Makeba.

A significant development came with the first Pride marches in South Africa, as the inaugural Johannesburg Pride was in 1990. Drag queens featured prominently in these early Pride parades, both as entertainers and as visible symbols of queerness. By the late 1990s, drag had become an accepted part of urban LGBTQ+ nightlife. In 1998, for example, a drag pageant was a highlight of the Pink Loerie Mardi Gras in Knysna, and Johannesburg's clubs were hosting weekly drag contests. Though challenges remained (conservative attitudes, risk of harassment, and racial divides within the gay community), South African drag artists of the 1990s laid the groundwork for today's thriving drag scene there. Drag was also a form of challenge to norms around race and gender. The 1990s in South Africa saw drag move from the fringes toward the spotlight, playing a significant part in the transformation of society.

INDIA: UNDERGROUND BEGINNINGS AND CULTURAL CONTEXT

In 1990s India, drag performance culture existed in a far more nascent and underground state compared to South Africa or the West. This was largely due to social and legal conditions; homosexuality was criminalised under Section 377, and overt queer expression (including drag) risked heavy stigma. Consensual gay sex was decriminalised only in 2018, overturning a judgement five years earlier that upheld the law. India has deep-rooted traditions of gender-crossing performance. For centuries, certain classical art forms have featured men in female roles; for example, Kathakali dance in Kerala or folk theatre like Yakshagana and Theyyam, where male performers wear elaborate female costumes and make-up (Desai & Shivlani 2024). These are respected cultural practices, not labelled as 'drag', but they indicate that the concept of gender non-conformity already strongly featured in Indian society. Moreover, the existence of the hijra community (India's transgender/non-binary community, who perform blessings or dances at weddings) meant that cross-gender expression had a traditional, though marginalised, place.

However, drag in terms of nightlife entertainment or queer activism was virtually invisible in public life during the 1990s. What drag scene did exist was largely confined to metro city gay circles and private parties. Mumbai and Delhi, for instance, had a small gay nightlife circuit in the late 1990s with some rare performances in drag. One early trailblazer was Bobby Darling (born Pankaj Sharma), who in the late 1990s left home in Delhi and moved to Mumbai to live openly as a trans woman. Darling found work performing at a Mumbai gay bar, working as a club showgirl, as well as securing roles in Bollywood films and later reality TV appearances in the 2000s. Darling's story denotes struggles in earlier life, to finally breaking into the entertainment industry. There were no established drag pageants or regular drag cabarets in the 1990s; someone like Darling had to invent a path largely alone, in a climate where gender non-conformity and transness was met with suspicion and hostile reactions.

It is important to note that while the 1990s lacked visible drag artists as celebrities, elements of drag *did* seep into Indian pop culture in other ways. Bollywood films occasionally featured male actors dressed as women for comic effect, which, while not true drag artistry, at least familiarised audiences with the sight of gender-bending. A prominent example is the film *Chachi 420* (1997), an Indian remake of *Mrs. Doubtfire*, in which actor Kamal Haasan spends most of the film convincingly made-up as an elderly female nanny. Millions of Indians laughed at the family comedy, perhaps not realising they were enjoying a form of drag performance. Such portrayals were usually positioned as farce, but they did contribute to slowly shifting perceptions. They also inadvertently inspired some budding drag artists. In fact, Alex Mathew, Maya the Drag Queen, who emerged in the 2010s, has said that watching *Mrs. Doubtfire* gave him the idea that performing as a woman could be thrilling (see also Chapter 3 for more on Maya the Drag Queen) (Upadhya 2017).

By the end of the 1990s, the first small LGBTQ+ support groups had formed in cities like Mumbai, Delhi, and Bangalore, and within these circles a few people toyed with drag. Examples include drag-themed house parties in Mumbai, where men would compete in sari contests behind closed doors. In Chennai and Tamil Nadu, the annual Koovagam festival was a gathering of thousands of hijra and trans people featuring beauty pageants. These pockets of activity were largely disconnected, but they set the stage for the 2000s, when Indian drag queens would gradually become more public in line with the legal progress for same-sex relationships. As Kannagi Desai and Mokshaa Shivlani (2024) put it, 'modern drag culture in India began to crystallise in the late twentieth century, heavily influenced by global trends yet deeply rooted in indigenous practices' (Desai & Shivlani 2024).

DRAG IN THE TWENTY-FIRST CENTURY: 2000 TO 2025

In the early 2000s, drag performers continued to hold court in the smoky pubs and clubs that had long nurtured and sustained their art. At the same time, a new setting was emerging: the digital realm (see Chapter 3). By the late 2000s, drag culture was still largely underground or unique to LGBTQ+ venues, yet online spaces meant a sense of global community was forming. Drag's popular culture profile rose in the West, but rich drag traditions and courageous new scenes also emerged across Asia, the Middle East, Africa, and Latin America. These communities often evolved under very different legal, political, social and cultural conditions, many in the face of intense opposition. Their stories between the 2000s–2020s underscore drag's global diversity and its power as an act of resistance.

The Beijing drag scene in China grew during the 2010s in semi-underground clubs like the Anchor Bar, where fortnightly shows drew raucous crowds despite the looming threat of authorities cracking down. Performers such as Lola Du Jour and Krystal de Canteur performed for LGBTQ+ audiences, even as they feared a government ban on 'sissy' or non-conforming gender expression (Poulsen Floris 2019). By 2019, Beijing's queens were 'throwing up high kicks…in light of the government's crackdown on gender performance', carving out a space for queer art in a rapidly changing society (Joe.s. 2019). In Shanghai and other Chinese cities, a drag 'boom' was noted by observers toward the end of the 2010s (Beiersdorfer 2022). In Japan, drag blended with a long history of gender-bending performance from Kabuki theatre to J-pop idols. Tokyo's Shinjuku neighbourhood has hosted drag shows for decades, notably at bars like Campy! and clubs where queens like Mitz Mangrove or Vivienne Sato entertain locals and tourists. Japan's drag culture often emphasises fashion and artistic polish, and some drag queens have become TV personalities. However, the scene represents incremental shifts in a society that is slowly opening up to LGBTQ+ visibility. South Korea saw the rise of drag in its tourist districts and university circles in the 2010s. Seoul now even hosts an annual Drag Parade, and Korean drag artists (for example, Nana Youngrong Kim, who appeared on a Netflix show called *Celebrity*) have used social media to gain support, though they too face opposition from conservative opponents.

Thailand is often understood to be the drag capital of Asia, as performers have long been part of the entertainment landscape. The country's famed *kathoey* (a term used to denote transgender women or sometimes conflated with 'drag' performers) hold cabaret shows in Bangkok and Pattaya, such as the glittering revues at Calypso Cabaret or Tiffany's Show. Essentially, this is a form of drag often aimed at tourists popularly known as 'ladyboy' shows. When *Drag Race Thailand* launched in 2018, it spotlighted queens like Annee Maywong and Natalia Pliacam who incorporated traditional Thai costumes and social messages, making an international audience take note of how drag can honour local heritage while pushing boundaries.

In the Philippines, drag has roots in pageant culture going back to the mid-twentieth century, where gay beauty contests provided both community entertainment and a rare space for LGBTQ+ expression (Del Mundo 2023). By the 2000s, Manila's club scene featured drag nights where queens performed both in glamorous

Filipiniana dresses and pop diva attire. The art form exploded in popularity recently thanks to shows like *Drag Race Philippines* (launched 2022) and the independent web series *La Más Draga* (which, though based in Mexico, inspired Filipino producers). The first *Drag Race Philippines* winner, Precious Paula Nicole, and performers like Xilhouete have become celebrated figures. They are able to use their platforms to make commentary on issues such as political corruption and religious conservatism – no small feat in a devoutly Catholic nation. In Singapore and Malaysia, drag shows exist mostly behind closed doors or in tourist bars due to strict laws, but performers like Singapore's Opera Tang or Malaysia's Cik Teh Botol have found creative ways to put on shows and build online followings, creating a drag presence that refused to be kept silent.

In parts of the Middle East, drag exists within vastly different sociopolitical landscapes. By the late 2010s, Beirut, long known for its nightlife, developed a small but vibrant drag circuit. Shows were typically announced discretely, with venues revealed only through word of mouth, and often held under tight secrecy and security (Loveluck 2019). Drag nights like the Grand Ball became a significant source of community and joy for LGBTQ+ people. Queens such as Anya Kneez, Diva Beirut, and Sultana led the way in drag performance in these contexts. In Tel Aviv, for instance, drag performers such as Miss Laila Carry are visible at Pride events and gay bars, pointing to a degree of cultural openness around LGBTQ+ expression. Yet, Shaka McGlotten raises significant points about how such visibility is extremely entangled with state and cultural politics in the region. In *Dragging: Or, In the Drag of a Queer Life*, McGlotten's research offers narrative portraits of drag performers, highlighting how drag performances expose critiques of Israeli exceptionalism (McGlotten 2021: 19). Elsewhere, McGlotten (2015) discusses the work of Liad Kantorowicz, described as 'a cis-gender woman who draws extensively on drag styles and idioms'. Kantorowicz's performance *Ain't No Democracy Here* challenges the 'mantra' of Israel as the only democracy in the Middle East by highlighting antidemocratic trends and state violence. McGlotten writes:

This mantra obscures and minimizes the extreme rightward shift in Israeli politics, which includes many antidemocratic trends, including laws penalizing calls for boycotts, restrictions on press freedoms, attacks on leftist NGOs, and the further politicization of the education system.

(McGlotten 2015)

In other regional contexts such as Egypt or the Gulf States, stories circulate of covert drag gatherings in cities like Dubai or Riyadh. Social media occasionally provides a platform for Middle Eastern drag artists, especially those in the diaspora, such as Iraqi-British performer Amrou Al-Kadhi (Glamrou), who writes about navigating drag and Islam (see also Chapter 2).

Latin America boasts some of the most dynamic drag cultures on the planet, often blending camp, telenovela drama, and political protest. In Brazil, drag has leapt from the clubs to the pop charts. Brazilian queen Pabllo Vittar became an international pop superstar in the late 2010s, breaking into Spotify's Global Top 50 and collaborating with major artists. Vittar was the first drag queen ever nominated for a Latin Grammy Award and accrued millions of fans, all while unapologetically singing about LGBTQ+ love and pride. Vittar's success includes headlining music festivals and starring in Adidas Pride campaigns (Malone Méndez 2020). In Mexico, drag's ingredients embrace indigenous and local flavours. The reality web series *La Más Draga*, launched in 2018 on YouTube, celebrates Mexican drag by incorporating cultural traditions and costumes. Mexico City's thriving scene, with clubs like Cabaretito and queens such as Deborah La Grande or Margaret Y Ya, often mixes Spanish and English songs, political satire about machismo, and sheer camp. In other Latin American countries, Chile had its own drag reality contest (*The Switch Drag Race*) as early as 2015. Argentina and Uruguay have cabaret traditions and drag artists (one Argentine drag performer, Dyhzy, is famously the child of the President of Argentina) (Rude & Lang 2019).

The pageant scene kept drag old-school: contour, coiffure, and cut-throat competition. Documentaries like *Pageant* (2008) spotlighted the Miss Gay America circuit, where Southern US drag thrived in church basements and veterans' halls. Andrew Logan's 'Alternative Miss World' was actually founded back in 1972. It is an anarchist take on the beauty pageant, where contestants of all genders compete in three categories: daywear, swimwear, and eveningwear. The judging deliberately refuses to focus on beauty, but instead focuses on transformation, creativity, artistry and originality. Icons such as Leigh Bowery and Derek Jarman helped turn the stage into a playground of imagination. The 'Alternative Miss World' is a jibe at pageantry, and has become a landmark in queer culture: a competition where being too much is just enough.

In the 2020s drag became more vibrant than ever, almost as if in direct protest to the glamour of drag. Alternative drag scenes rebelled against what they saw as the *Drag Race* mould and factory. With alt artists, drag is purposefully radical, political, or shocking. Its intention is to sit in stark contrast to drag's mainstream palpability. The rise of the show *Dragula*, created by the Boulet Brothers in 2016, epitomises this counter current. Marketed with the slogan 'Dragula is not pretty', it celebrates horror, filth, and glamour in equal measure (Apichatsakol 2021). Contestants on *Dragula* might pour fake blood over themselves, transform into zombies or alien creatures, or perform high-concept performance art pieces onstage. The show includes drag kings, transgender and non-binary performers, and others often excluded from mainstream drag pageantry. In 2019, *Dragula* crowned Landon Cider, a drag king, making history as the first AFAB (assigned-female-at-birth) drag performer to win a drag competition show. Alt drag insists on challenging drag's norms, often returning it to its activist roots of radical protest.

DRAG IN THE TIME OF COVID-19

In 2020, the COVID-19 pandemic brought with it enforced lockdowns and restrictions around social distancing that proved incredibly challenging to drag's industries. Drag's response required ingenuity, alongside careful navigation and negotiation. The pandemic also brought heartache to the drag world. Performers fell ill; some, like Nashom Wooden (known as drag queen Mona Foot of NYC), tragically died from the virus in the early days. Drag's economy had largely depended on populating crowded bars, and, without in-person events, artists struggled to earn. Yet, drag's core resilience rose to the challenge. Artists embraced the age-old entertainment slogan, 'the show must go on'. When Pride 2020 events were cancelled, drag performers set up virtual parades and online charity fundraisers. They read storybooks to kids over Zoom (continuing drag queen story hour virtually) through spaces like Brooklyn

Library and Sonoma County Library; and they hosted countless charity live-streams for causes like food banks and bail funds, leveraging their talents for community support. By 2021 and 2022, as venues gradually reopened, audiences and performers had new tools in their arsenal, ready to embrace digital drag (see Chapter 3).

THREATS AND RESILIENCE IN THE 2020S

Gentrification is the process where poor urban areas are taken over by wealthy investors, driving local people away and making housing unaffordable. Sadly, this has impacted a number of queer venues and locations. A quieter challenge to drag in the twenty-first century has been the closure of LGBTQ+ venues, often due to gentrification and economic pressure. These are the very spaces that give us many of our drag histories. To provide some scale of this, half of London's gay bars closed between 2006 and 2017 (Campkin & Marshall 2017) and about a third of queer bars in the USA shuttered in a similar time frame (Russell 2022). Rent hikes, property development, and the changing habits of younger generations (who might socialise more online or in mixed spaces) all contributed to this decline.

We now bear witness to a current uprooting of history in London, UK, as several drag and queer venues are being threatened with precarity or closure due to financial pressures. Tim Brunsden's *Save the Tavern* (2017) documentary uses media to spotlight the threat of closure of the legendary Royal Vauxhall Tavern (RVT) (Brunsden 2015). Academic and activist Ben Walters has also campaigned against the threat of closure of the RVT. Walters wrote an application to Historic England in the hope of saving the RVT from property developers. His bid was successful and the RVT became the first listed building for its importance to LGBTQ+ histories (see Walters 2021).

Impoverished urban regions have also become a settlement for gentrification, and this process has meant that poorer LGBTQ+ inhabitants have had to relocate from their place of dwelling. Christopher Street in New York City has seen a surge in gentrification, causing drag and queer people of colour to relocate from what was once their home and neighbourhood to make way for white middle- and upper-class wealth. Sarah Schulman (2012) delves into the increase in gentrification during the 1980s and 1990s, giving an insider account of how queer culture, vibrant cutting-edge arts scenes and inexpensive properties were erased by mainstream consumerism. 'Gaybourhoods' (primarily gay regions) mainly became 'heterohoods' (straight environments). Peter Moskowitz, in his text *How to Kill a City: Gentrification, Inequality, and the Fight for the Neighborhood* (2017), also writes on gentrification, centring discussion on financial affordability and highlighting the 'who cans' and 'who can'ts' in the USA. This is starkly linked to race inequalities. These stories are not unique to the UK and USA; they form part of a wider narrative impacting drag and queer spaces through a slow drip eradication that is, unfortunately, sweeping through many places.

We only need to take a glance at the current climate of anti-drag protesters that are prevalent on the internet and a swarm of anti-drag bills that is bringing about legislation to ban, or limit, drag in public spaces to speculate on how further marginalised queer and drag spaces will become. Tennessee has passed the first law in the USA limiting drag shows. It passed laws that broadly banned 'adult-oriented performances' (with drag explicitly named), although portions of such laws were challenged in courts as unconstitutional. Oklahoma also passed a law, while Kentucky, Arizona, and several other states have also proposed bills prohibiting male or female impersonation (drag) under the banner of adult cabaret. Sadly, drag's progress faces challenges by those who seek to reverse it.

This pushback is fuelled by 'drag panic', a belief that exposure to drag is harmful to children. Sociologist Stanley Cohen coined the term 'moral panic' in his 1972 study *Folk Devils and Moral Panics* to denote an irrational fear or concern that an individual or group may pose to the values of society. The reason it is a 'panic' is because the response is typically disproportionate to the actual threat, fuelled by sensationalist media coverage and political rhetoric. Drag panic follows this pattern, with drag performers being perceived as a threat to the 'innocence' of children without any evidence, simply for reading stories to them. . The amplification of this panic increases through media coverage, and people accept generic assertions without analysing for detail and evidence.

Just as drag achieved unprecedented visibility across the globe, it has been met with a mounting fierce backlash. From 2010 to the present, there is a worrying rise in threats to drag performance, including reactionary legislation noted above, to organised harassment and protest outside of performance spaces. As can be seen through this chapter, the paradox of rise and resistance has historical antecedents. Periods of queer progress are often met with conservative counter-movements. This resistance is prejudiced and discriminatory; it is hate and violence masked as free speech. In June 2022 a group of five men (known as Proud Boys) stormed into San Lorenzo Library in California's San Francisco Bay Area, with the intention of causing disruption to drag queen story hour. The men shouted homophobic and transphobic slurs at the drag queens. The event was so aggressive and upsetting to the drag artists, as well as the children present, that it prompted a hate-crime investigation (Goodyear 2022). Similar incidents are occurring with alarming frequency.

Yet the threat is clear: some in power want drag back behind closed doors, or gone altogether. Globally, this legislative push echoes existing restrictions on drag in many countries. For instance, Russia's 2013 'gay propaganda' law had already made drag essentially illegal by banning positive depictions of LGBTQ+ lifestyles to minors. And Uganda's 2023 anti-LGBTQ+ law is among the harshest in the world, criminalising gender non-conformity, thereby putting drag performers at dire risk. In terms of protest and activism, there is still much work to do, as Chapter 2 goes on to detail.

FURTHER READING

Baker, R. (1968). *Drag: A History of Female Impersonation in the Performing Arts*. **London: Triton Books.** One of the earliest texts that traces the form of drag herstories. Baker documents the history of female impersonation across theatre, vaudeville, cabaret, and screen. While language and ideas about drag have moved on, this is an early source that set the basis for writing and researching about drag pasts.

Bloomfield, J. (2023). *Drag: A British History*. **Oakland, CA: University of California Press.** Bloomfield's book takes a deep dive into the often-overlooked corners of British drag history. With the tenacity of a queen rummaging for vintage sequins, this well-researched text charts the evolution of drag from the music halls to the modern-day spotlight. It is essential reading for anyone wanting to understand British drag performance.

Drysdale, K. (2019). *Intimate Investments in Drag King Cultures: The Rise and Fall of a Lesbian Social Scene*. **Cham, Switzerland: Palgrave Macmillan.** Drysdale focuses in on Sydney's drag kinging scene with academic attention. Covering the years 1999–2012, this ethnographic text offers real first-hand accounts of drag king cultures. It is a refreshing and critical read for those researching subcultural performance and queer night-life beyond queen narratives that dominate.

Edward, M. & Farrier, S. (eds) (2021). *Drag Histories, Herstories and Hairstories: Drag in a Changing Scene Volume 2.* **London: Bloomsbury.** This is an academic collection of essays exploring various periods of drag history. Drawing on case studies, archives, and creative methodologies, the book offers what the editors call a 'sequin method' to drag history/herstory: some stories sparkle brightly, others remain hidden or muted.

Ferris, L. (ed.). (1993). *Crossing the Stage: Controversies on Cross-Dressing.* **London: Routledge.** This collection takes a theatrical trip through time, from toga-draped Romans to the ruffled sleeves of ballet. With case studies of cross-dressing through history, Ferris' volume is a key text for understanding gender performance and theatre.

Halberstam, J. (1998). *Female Masculinity.* **Durham NC: Duke University Press.** Halberstam's landmark text flips the script on what masculinity can look like through sharp analysis and cultural commentary focussed on research with and about drag kings.

Into the Limelight. (n.d.). Male Impersonators. Retrieved from https://intothelimelight.org/category/male-impersonators. An overview of historical male impersonators in the UK.

Lawrence, T. & Regnault, C. (2011). *Voguing and the House Ballroom Scene of New York City 1989–92.* **London: Soul Jazz Books.** Through its iconic ballroom realness, this book captures the magic of late 1980s/early 1990s New York ballroom culture. With stunning photography, it invites you into a world of houses, categories, and fierce voguing.

Newton, E. (1972). *Mother Camp: Female Impersonators in America.* **Englewood Cliffs, NJ: Prentice-Hall.** Based on fieldwork in the late 1960s, this book is one of the earlier key contributions to the study of drag performers in the United States. Through interviews and observations, Newton explores the social worlds of drag in bars and clubs. While the language of the time may now feel dated, the book offers valuable insights into drag.

Rupp, L. J. & Taylor, V. (2003). *Drag Queens and the 801 Cabaret Bar.* **Chicago, IL: University of Chicago Press.** Engaging with first-hand interviews and observations with Florida's 801 Cabaret, the authors combine oral histories, archival research, and cultural analysis to capture how drag became political, communal, and entertaining.

Senelick, L. (2000). *The Changing Room: Sex, Drag and Theatre.* **London: Routledge.** This book offers comprehensive history of drag performance from ancient to modern theatre. Senelick traces drag's roots in the theatre, through detailed archival research, assessment of performance records, and cultural analysis, Senelick explores a number of forms: Shakespearean drama, Kabuki, burlesque, and into contemporary performance.

Tennant, J. (2022). *It's a Drag: Cross-Dressing in Performance.* **Lanham, MD: Applause Theatre and Cinema Books.** Tennant details the history of cross-dressing traditions in performance, from Greek tragedy to pantomime dames and wartime drag. This is an accessible read that also questions the language of the past ('cross-dressing' included) and gestures toward a more nuanced understanding of gender play in performance.

Volcano, D. L. G. & Halberstam, J. (1999). *The Drag King Book.* **London: Serpent's Tail.** Equal parts photo album, performance archive, and gender manifesto, this book is a bold celebration of drag king culture. Volcano's striking photography meets Halberstam's sharp prose to document drag kings in the late 1990s.

GLOSSARY

AFAB   Assigned female at birth.

Apartheid   A system of racial segregation and discrimination enforced by the South African government from 1948 to the early 1990s, where people were separated by race and South Africans of colour were denied basic rights.

Ballroom culture   A subculture, especially in Black and Latinx LGBTQ+ communities, where people compete in drag or dance categories in 'balls'.

Camp   An artistic style that embraces exaggeration, humour, and theatricality.

Cisnormativity   The assumption that everyone is cisgender (identifies with the sex they were assigned at birth).

Cross-dressing   Wearing clothes traditionally associated with a different gender.

Dandy   A man concerned with physical appearance, personal grooming, refined language and leisurely hobbies associated with wealth.

Gender binary   The rigid classification of gender into two distinct, opposite forms: male and female.

Gender fluidity   The idea that gender is not fixed and can change over time.

Gender non-conforming   Someone whose gender expression does not match society's expectations.

Herstory   A feminist term meaning 'her story', used instead of 'history' to highlight women's or marginalised people's perspectives.

Heteronormativity   The belief or assumption that everyone is straight and that heterosexuality is the norm.

Hijra   A traditional third gender in South Asia, often involving people assigned male at birth who live as women or non-binary individuals.

Kathoey   often translated as 'ladyboy' but can include trans women or gender non-conforming people.

LGBTQ+   An abbreviation for lesbian, gay, bisexual, transgender, queer/questioning, and others. It includes a range of gender and sexual identities.

Minstrelsy/Blackface   A form of racist entertainment where white performers painted their faces to imitate and mock Black people.

Misogynoir   A specific kind of discrimination that targets Black women, combining racism and sexism.

Misogyny   Hatred or prejudice against women.

Molly Houses   Secret meeting places in eighteenth- and nineteenth-century Britain where bisexual, gay and gender non-conforming men would gather socially.

Onnagata   In traditional Japanese Kabuki theatre, a male actor who plays female roles.

Pantomime Dame   A British theatre tradition representing drag in a silly, over-the-top costume, often in Christmas performances.

Patriarchy   A society or system where men hold power and women are excluded or undervalued.

Queer   A reclaimed word used by some LGBTQ+ people to describe their identities. It can also refer to theories that challenge traditional ideas of gender and sexuality.

Restoration period   A time in British history (starting in 1660) when the monarchy was restored and theatre became more open, allowing women to perform on stage.

Section 377   A British colonial law that criminalised homosexuality in India and other countries.

Sequin method   A metaphor for drag history research, where some stories sparkle more brightly than others, but all are part of the whole (see Edward & Farrier 2022).

Toff   A term used by lower classes to refer to the British upper classes.

Two-Spirit   A modern term used by some Indigenous North Americans to describe people with both masculine and feminine spirits, often with unique social or spiritual roles.

Vaudeville/Music Hall   Popular forms of variety entertainment in the nineteenth and early twentieth centuries that included singing, dancing, and comedy, often with drag acts.

REFERENCES

Apichatsakol, M. (2021). 'Dragula: Showcasing an Alternative Side of Drag Artistry'. Retrieved from www.koktailmagazine.com/2021/11/21/dragula (accessed June 2025).

Baker, R. A. (2022). *British Music Hall: An Illustrated History*. Barnsley: Pen and Sword.

Beiersdorfer, R. (2022). 'Such a Tease: Beijing Queen Velvet Teese Strips Gender Norms'. The China Temper. Retrieved from https://chinatemper.com/the-series/drag-divas/drag-queen-velvet-teese (accessed June 2025).

Bloomfield, J. (2021). 'Soldiers in Skirts: Cross-Dressing Ex-Servicemen, Sexuality and Censorship in Post-War Britain'. In Edward, M. & Farrier, S. (eds), *Drag Histories, Herstories and Hairstories: Drag in a Changing Scene Volume 2*, 41–55. London: Bloomsbury.

Bloomfield, J. (2023). *Drag: A British History*. Oakland, CA: University of California Press.

Brady, C. (2024). 'Camp Sensibility and Gay Licence in the Mainstream: A Critical Analysis of the phenomenon/subculture of the British Northern Fun Pub Circa 1973–1993'. PhD thesis, retrieved from https://research.edgehill.ac.uk/en/studentTheses/camp-sensibility-and-gay-licence-in-the-mainstream.

Brunsden, T. (2015). 'Save the Tavern'. Retrieved from https://www.light-factory.co.uk/save-the-tavern (accessed June 2025).

Campkin, B. & Marshall, L. (2017). 'LGBTQ+ Cultural Infrastructure in London: Night Venues, 2006–Present'. UCL. Retrieved from www.ucl.ac.uk/bartlett/sites/bartlett/files/LGBTQ_cultural_infrastructure_in_London_nightlife_venues_2006_to_the_present.pdf (accessed June 2025).

Cohen, S. (1972). *Folk Devils and Moral Panics*. London: Routledge.

De Barros, L. (2015). 'Dainti Delischia: A South African Drag Legend Passes on'. MambaOnline. Retrieved from https://www.mambaonline.com/2015/05/13/dainti-delicia-south-african-drag-legend-passes/ (accessed June 2025).

de Choisy, F. T. (1920). *Mémoires de l'abbé de Choisy habillé en femme*. Project Gutenberg. Retrieved from https://editions-sillage.fr/wp-content/uploads/2020/04/9791091896320_memoires_de_l_abbe_de_choisy_habille_en_femme_editions_sillage_2015.pdf (accessed June 2025).

Del Mundo, Z. (2023). 'BAKLAsin ang Kinagawian: The Ever-Evolving Artistry of Filipino Drag Performance and Queer Art'. UPLB Perspective. Retrieved from https://uplbperspective.wordpress.com/2023/07/17/baklasin-ang-kinagawian-the-ever-evolving-artistry-of-filipino-drag-performance-and-queer-art (accessed June 2025).

Desai, K. & Shivlani, M. (2024). 'The Rise and Influence of Drag Culture in India, with the Queens (and Kings) in the Spotlight'. Elle. Retrieved from https://elle.in/rise-and-influence-of-drag-culture-in-india (accessed June 2025).

Doonan, S. (2019). *Drag: The Complete Story*. London, UK: Laurence King Publishing.

Drysdale, K. (2019). *Intimate Investments in Drag King Cultures: The Rise and Fall of a Lesbian Social Scene*. Cham, Switzerland: Palgrave Macmillan.

Edward, M. & Farrier, S. (eds) (2021). *Drag Histories, Herstories and Hairstories: Drag in a Changing Scene Volume 2*. London: Bloomsbury.

Farrier, S. (2021). 'Kinging the Stage: Male Impersonators and Drag Kings, Exploring Shared Historical Narratives'. In Edward, M. & Farrier, S. (eds), *Drag Histories, Herstories and Hairstories: Drag in a Changing Scene Volume 2*, 57–68. London: Bloomsbury.

First Hand Films. (2014). 'Man for a Day'. Retrieved from https://vimeo.com/ondemand/manforaday (accessed June 2025).

Gabrovska, G. (2020). 'Performance of Gendered Bodies'. In Holca, I. & Tămaş, C. (eds), *Forms of the Body in Contemporary Japanese Society, Literature, and Culture*, 49–72. Lanham, MD: Lexington Books.

Geilhorn, B. (2017). 'Women in a Man's World: Gender and Power in Japanese Noh Theatre'. In Madhavan, A. (ed.), *Women in Asian Performance*, 28–38. Abingdon: Routledge.

Gibson, J. L. (2000). *Squeaking Cleopatras: the Elizabethan Boy Player*. Stroud: Sutton Publishing.

Goodyear, S. (2022). 'Drag Queen Keeps Reading to Kids after Group of Men Disrupt Pride Event Yelling Slurs'. CBC Radio. Retrieved from www.cbc.ca/radio/asithappens/as-it-happens-monday-edition-1.6486762/drag-queen-keeps-reading-to-kids-after-group-of-men-disrupt-pride-event-yelling-slurs-1.6488356 (accessed June 2025)

Hills, C. (2013). 'Mandela's Love for Humor Was on Full Display When He Sat for an Interview with "Evita"'. The World from PRX. Retrieved from https://theworld.org/stories/2013/12/12/pieter-dirk-uys-mandelas-love-satire (accessed June 2025).

Joe.s. (2019). 'Being in the East is Such a Drag'. Ezra Temko. Retrieved from https://ezratemko.com/drag/being-in-the-east-is-such-a-drag (accessed June 2025).

Kirk, K. & Heath, E. (1984). *Men in Frocks*. London: GMP Publishers.

Loveluck, L. (2019). 'Beirut's Fearless Drag Queens Defy Middle Eastern Conservatism'. *The Washington Post*, 26 January. Retrieved from https://www.washingtonpost.com/world/beiruts-fearless-drag-queens-belie-middle-eastern-conservatism/2019/01/26/2a7abcd4-ffb7-11e8-a17e-162b712e8fc2_story.html (accessed June 2025).

Malone Méndez, C. (2020). 'Pabllo Vittar's Multilingual Music Is, Above All, a Gift to Her Fans'. NPR Music. Retrieved from https://www.forbes.com/sites/cmalone/2020/04/30/pabllo-vittars-multilingual-music-is-above-all-a-gift-to-her-fans/ (accessed June 2025).

McGlotten, S. (2015). 'The Political Aesthetics of Drag'. *Metropolitics*, 13 October. Retrieved from https://metropolitiques.eu/IMG/pdf/met-mcglotten.pdf (accessed June 2025).

McGlotten, S. (2021). *Dragging: Or, In the Drag of a Queer Life*. New York: Routledge.

Moskowitz, P. E. (2017). *How to Kill a City: Gentrification, Inequality, and the Fight for the Neighborhood*. New York: Bold Type Books.

National Archives (2021). '"Queer" History: A History of Queer'. Retrieved from https://blog.nationalarchives.gov.uk/queer-history-a-history-of-queer (accessed June 2025).

Newley, P. (2007). *The Amazing Mrs Shufflewick: The Life and Times of Rex Jameson*. London: Third Age Press.

Nissinen, M. (1998). *Homoeroticism in the Biblical World: A Historical Perspective*. Minneapolis, MN: Fortress Press.

Norton, R. (1992). *Mother Clap's Molly House: The Gay Subculture in England 1700–1830*. London: Gay Men's Press.

Oremland, P. (dir.). (1984). *If They'd Asked For a Lion Tamer*. TV documentary, Channel 4, broadcast 5 April.

Paulson, D. & Simpson, R. (1996). *An Evening at the Garden of Allah: A Gay Cabaret in Seattle*. New York: Columbia University Press.

Poulsen Floris, L. (2019). 'Drag Queens of Beijing Strut Their Stuff While They Can, Fearing a Chinese Government Crackdown'. South China Morning Post, 17 February. Retrieved from https://www.scmp.com/lifestyle/arts-culture/article/2186000/drag-queens-beijing-strut-their-stuff-while-they-can-fearing (accessed June 2025).

Radcliffe, C. (2011). 'Dan Leno: Dame of Drury Lane'. In David, J. (ed.), *Victorian Pantomime: A Collection of Critical Essays*, 118–134. London: Palgrave Macmillan.

Rude, M. & Lang, N. (2019). 'Argentina's Next President Loves His Drag Queen Son'. Out. Retrieved from www.out.com/drag/2019/11/04/argentinas-next-president-loves-his-drag-queen-son (accessed June 2025).

Russell, J. (2022). 'Gay Bars Are on the Decline Nationwide According to New Study'. LGBTQ Nation. Retrieved from https://www.lgbtqnation.com/2022/06/gay-bars-decline-nationwide-according-new-study/ (accessed June 2025).

Schulman, S. (2012). *The Gentrification of the Mind: Witness to a Lost Imagination*. Berkeley, CA: University of California Press.

Sculthorpe, D. (2022). *Malcolm Scott-The Woman Who Knows*. Orlando, FL: BearManor Media.

Slide, A. (1986). *Great Pretenders: A History of Female and Male Impersonation in the Performing Arts*. Lombard, IL: Wallace-Homestead Book Company.

Upadhya, R. (2017). 'Being Gay Is Illegal in India, but that Doesn't Stop These Drag Queens'. Vice India. Retrieved from www.vice.com/sv/article/being-gay-is-illegal-in-india-but-that-doesnt-stop-these-drag-queens (accessed June 2025).

Walters, B. (2021). '"Once Upon a Time, There Was a Tavern": Metadrag and Other Uses of the Past at the Royal Vauxhall Tavern'. In Edward, M. & Farrier, S. (eds), *Drag Histories, Herstories and Hairstories: Drag in a Changing Scene Volume 2*, 15–28. London: Bloomsbury.

Ward, E. (1709). *The History of the London Clubs, Or, The Citizens' Pastime*. London: J. Dutten.

DRAG THEORY, PRACTICE, AND ACTIVISM

INTRODUCTION

The chapter provides a basic introduction to key concepts in gender/queer theory and theories of representation and intersectionality. The chapter then explores these issues in practice, in relation to activism specifically. The chapter is structured in three sections:

1   drag in theory;
2   drag in practice;
3   drag and activism.

Therefore, the reader is encouraged to read each section alongside one another, given that academics often reflect on activism, including documenting the events and their social, cultural, political and legislative import. And, activist activities can be academic, too, through teaching and research *by*, *with*, and *for* marginalised groups.

   The first section traces a basic history by which drag cultures have come to be examined in academic contexts, through a critical and rich relationship with feminist, postmodern and queer thought. The section explores the evolution of research and literature relating to critical theories such as feminism, queer theory, gender performativity, and intersectionality. The aim of this section is to offer an overview of the theorisation of drag within academic studies, including an accessible summary to the theoretical perspectives. These theories have been formed over many years of activism and protest, both inside and outside of the academy. Queer theory exposes how normative understandings of gender and sexuality only

DOI: 10.4324/9781003431800-3

relate to cisgender identities and heterosexuality. It therefore calls for disruptive methods which allow non-heterosexual and gender non-conforming people to be visible, and drag is often considered the example par excellence of gender non-conformity.

In exploring how drag intersects with other markers of identity in varying ways, the second section offers overviews of some of the key issues and concepts relating to LGBTQ+ rights, the tensions surrounding visibility and representation of drag kings and drag queens, drag and misogyny, drag and racism, and drag and disability.

As a visible, in-your-face representation of queer life, drag has been both leading and supporting activist activities across a range of political issues, including those affecting the LGBTQ+ community, specifically, as well as broader, global issues.

The final section of this chapter offers an exploration of activist case studies related to the following political themes: LGBTQ+ rights; gender-based violence and #MeToo; religion and activism; advocacy for sexual health; awareness raising for mental health and climate change. In this way, drag is more than entertainment; it is part of wider activist anti-racist movements, protests, consciousness-raising and advocacy.

DRAG IN THEORY

KEY IDEAS

To date, there is no such drag theory. Drag has always been a magpie activity: borrowing, parodying, impersonating. In fact, if you search for the keywords 'drag' and 'theory' in academic search engines, you will find references to physics and engineering concerned with the impact of force on an object! As there is no explicit theory, drag has been used to think about aspects of gender, sexualities and social inclusion across a range of subjects. The starting point has always been on the practice and performance of drag. People interested in drag have usually come to it from both social and cultural perspectives: through media and TV shows, drag bars, socialising and other cultural activities. The focus of drag therefore has always been a *practice* first and foremost, rather than being an outcome of a theory around gender and sexualities. For those who research drag for academic purposes, the focus has often been on practice too. We see this in the recent journal articles, books and scholarly texts on drag, including the explicit focus on practice in the volumes edited by Edward and Farrier (2020, 2021, 2025). A small number of these texts are referenced in this chapter, and, for readers wanting to pursue their interests further, the items in the reference list serve as a useful starting point. Therefore, and in sharp contrast to the age-old question about the chicken and the egg, we come to the realisation that drag practices have always existed (see Chapter 1) and their existence has predated, and therefore, informed, theoretical ideas and concepts. Indeed, for those familiar with academic processes, it is rather rare for the practice to come before theory, except in practice-research methodologies used in the creative and performing arts. This has been a popular lens underpinning performance and creative based research.

Drag has often been used as an example of disruption to normative gender presentations. Normative in this sense does not mean 'normal'. Rather, it points to the idea of gender presentation as behavioural, in a binary model of women's appearance being considered feminine (and its association with certain types of hair styles, clothing, make-up, shoes, accessories) and male appearance denoting masculinity (with similar stereotypical associations). In disrupting what is commonly seen as masculine/feminine or male/female, drag is therefore linked to alternative, non-normative representation. Drag researchers ought to remember that drag is interdisciplinary and therefore a gate-crasher to ideas found in all disciplines in the arts, humanities and social sciences. Although drag may find its kin within performance and creative arts studies, it still resists being boxed into neat academic disciplines and can be found in a range of other, often surprising, studies.

FEMINISM, QUEER THEORY, AND GENDER PERFORMATIVITY

Thinking and conceptualising about and around drag in academia has often found its grounding in queer theory. Queer theory did not appear in the 1990s out of nowhere, and its evolution is indebted to feminism. Therefore, a very concise history of feminism is needed to understand the resistance to male domination and heteronormativity in legal, political, social, and cultural activities that later came to characterise queer theory. Such activities paved the way to challenge inequalities, and later, the continuous disruption of the status quo. Feminist theory begins by giving critical attention to the gendered norms and inequalities of socialisation.

As we grow up, we learn rules and how to behave in different ways depending on the various settings we are in and the people around us. There is much diversity across the globe in how humans behave – some cultures have customs that can be different, even strange to others. Therefore, our behaviours are individual activities that impact on others. Each of the behaviours we become aware of and enact are part of a process called socialisation. Socialisation varies across time (how things change throughout history), cultures, and in different geographical locations. It is partly through our socialisation in behaviours and contexts that we construct language, a sense of who we are and our behaviours. We can share these identities with others.

While our behaviour is interpreted by others and therefore draws a response from them, in turn, others' reactions are also something that determine and regulate our behaviour. We learn how *not* to behave in certain areas; we are encouraged to separate private and public behaviours, individual and professional ones. There is a social script of rules that determines what is permitted and what is frowned upon. With explicit focus on gender and sexuality, this social script has been vastly determined by patriarchy and heteronormativity, described below. There are other privileged characteristics that shape social scripts, including class, ableism, race/ethnicity, religion – all dependent on what has become the dominant set of ideas and beliefs over time. In theoretical terms, we speak of ideology to describe this system of ideas, beliefs and behaviours.

Patriarchy has been the dominant social system that privileges men throughout history. Traditionally men have had and exercised privilege over women. This has resulted in gender inequalities that still exist today. Patriarchy has meant that men have controlled all aspects of religious, legal, social, political and cultural life, exerting strong influence over the actions of women. The system of patriarchy has existed throughout history. Indeed, we see numerous examples of patriarchal men exercising control over women in ancient religious texts such as the Torah, the Qur'an, and the Bible. Such texts are still used to render women subordinate in some religious traditions and societies. Patriarchy is still problematic; it still has a disturbing legacy and impact today.

Thankfully, feminist activities have shone light on damaging patriarchal practices, and fought for gender equalities. In theoretical terms, the study of feminism has been considered in 'waves'. Initially, feminist activism and protest sought equal rights in law, through the Suffragette movement in the UK, which resulted in securing the vote for women and women's rights to own property. This forms the first 'wave' of feminism, that began in the mid-nineteenth century to post-World War II, approximately. In the Western world, the second wave can be linked to the 1950s–1960s, and this period represents a move for women and feminists to debate a wider range of issues including sexuality, reproductive rights, family life, and the workplace. The second wave is thought to have lasted approximately two decades, in which it drew attention to institutional sexism and sought to right existing inequalities at the time.

This second wave of feminism is an exciting time for academic theory, and during this period we see feminist thinking infiltrate academic disciplines: literature, sociology, arts, humanities. A pioneer to some of the second wave thinking can be found in the pivotal text *The Second Sex* by French philosopher Simone de Beauvoir (first published in 1949). De Beauvoir famously claims that 'one is not born a woman; one becomes a woman'; she cites man as the default, and woman as 'other'. De Beauvoir's claim shed light on how ideas of 'woman' are socially constructed – that girls and women were thought of in terms of their fertility and familial function, as mothers and wives. Girls were socially constructed to engage in gender play during childhood, in activities that simulated cleaning, washing, cooking, caring for toys, and all of these games serve as practice for future home-making activities and, consequently, a woman's function in domestic life. Employment was typically gendered, with women entering professions associated with their presumed skills of care-giving and nurture, such as teaching and nursing. De Beauvoir spotlighted how a collective male social objective was to keep patriarchy intact through the subordination of women.

The third wave of feminism is situated in the 1990s, instigated by those who had embraced the feminist attitudes of their mothers' and parents' generation, and found much more work to do. During the third wave, feminists questioned other structural inequalities that led to multiple marginalisation of women, including around identity characteristics such as race/ethnicity, class, and sexuality.

Here, intersectional approaches begin to emerge (more below). To conclude the overview of feminist waves, the fourth wave of feminism began in approximately 2012, and here digital activism has played an essential role in focussing attention on sexual violence, rape culture, and body shaming experiences of women. The most prominent example of this can be seen in the use of the #MeToo hashtag to draw attention to the widespread sexual violence and assault experienced by girls and women worldwide.

This very abridged history of feminist theory and activism helps set out the social and cultural backdrop to the contexts in which LGBTQ+ rights emerged. In a theoretical sense, scholarship that was based on women's experiences, particularly during the second and third waves, also paid due attention to sexuality.

A significant essay that can be seen as a pre-cursor to the emergence of queer theory is Adrienne's Rich's 'Compulsory Heterosexuality and Lesbian Identity' (1980). Rich's essay examined heterosexuality through a critical lens, describing and analysing its role as a major social power. According to Rich, people are socialised into understanding how heterosexuality is the norm, and people therefore conform to the rules of heterosexuality. Rich's paper was concerned with lesbian visibility within feminist literature, and it was a challenge to previous feminist studies as it drew attention to how non-heterosexuality had not received much airtime. Rich exposed how non-heterosexuality is organised, imposed and policed by society, and she challenges the power structures in which this operates. Those who deviate, and do not play by the rules, experience losses. This can be seen in the experiences of homophobia and biphobia for those who identify as non-heterosexual, or transphobia and queerphobia for those who are non-cisgender. Heterosexuality was therefore compulsory.

In 1991, Michael Warner coined the now commonly used term 'heteronormativity' to describe the notion that heterosexuality is the standard of sexuality. Although Warner's use of the term was unique to him, the idea that heterosexuality was 'compulsory' can be traced back to Rich's earlier work. So, while heterosexuality had been on the radar of feminist and women's studies for some time through the emergence of queer theory, the notion of compulsory heterosexuality was shattered. Queer theory resisted the prioritisation of heterosexuality, and created a space for a number of queer identities. We see how academic terms such as heteronorma-tivity have become common place in discussions around LGBTQ+ rights today. They have also given rise to similar terms, such as 'cisnormativity' to describe how normative ideologies about gender have become so dominant. This term is commonly used to describe how someone's gender identity matches their biological sex, or sex assigned at birth.

Feminist thinking therefore provides a fertile playground in which gender trouble can occur. This trouble takes the form of queer the-ory. Queer theory is the rogue, rebellious, revolutionary offspring of feminism. Its emergence coincides with third wave feminism, but its focus takes a different direction.

A QUEER THEORY IS BORN ...

The birth of queer theory, therefore, has a rich ancestry in feminist thought, and in LGBTQ+ activism. Long before its use as a bold identity marker, the term 'queer' was used as a term of abuse. There is a distinction between how homophobic people use the term as derogatory, to how LGBTQ+ people use the term themselves. The homophobic slur was reclaimed by activists who used slogans such as 'We're here, we're queer, get used to it!' on the streets of New York in the 1990s in protests for lesbian, gay and bisexual rights as well as HIV/AIDS activism. The term 'queer' has been reclaimed and its popular usage attests to this. In addition to its use as an identity marker for non-normative gender/sexualities, its use in the academy can be traced back to the 1990s also.

The term 'queer theory' is attributed to Teresa de Lauretis, who ran a conference using that term in its title in 1990. This led to a special issue of the journal *Differences: A Journal of Feminist Cultural Studies*, entitled 'Queer Theory: Lesbian and Gay Sexualities'. Indeed, at the time of its coinage and first use, queer theory was concerned with lesbian, gay and bisexual identities. Queer the-ory helped to explain and spotlight how structures of power were wrapped up in heterosexuality.

Judith Butler's pivotal text *Gender Trouble* (1990) is one that uses and exposes drag as the disruptive marker of gender *par excellence*. Butler's work has been considered and critiqued for its high level of theorisation and complexity. In a nutshell, queer theory refuses to see gender and sexuality as fixed identities. Instead, they are social constructions, which are regulated and policed through social and cultural ideas, behaviours and expectations. So rather than being a fixed, innate, or natural aspect of our physical make-up, gender is considered performative through our enactments.

In these terms, therefore, there is a distinction between sex and gender. Sex is associated with genitalia, chromosomes, hormones, and reproductive organs. Gender is concerned with roles, behaviours and identities that are constructed by society and is, accordingly, associated with ideas of what is masculine or feminine. Gender has been considered as performative within a limited two-model system that has dominated throughout time. In academic theory, we speak about gender *performativity* to highlight that individuals have little choice in how they enact gender. 'Performativity' differs from 'performance' – when individuals enact gender, they are not acting in a theatrical sense, but rather expressing their authentic selves. Conversely, they may be expressing themselves in terms of expectations of gender, through a form of masking wherein one can find safety.

Gender performativity is a communal enterprise, in that we begin to associate and attribute ideas relating to binary positions of masculine and feminine with these enactments. Contemporary examples see pink associated with the birth of a girl, and blue for a boy. Skirts can be found in girls' and women's wear departments, while ties will be located in men's wear. Across the globe, clothing, appearance and accessories are all neatly categorised into binary gender: male and female. Yet while this neatness may suit and privilege some, it is entirely restrictive for those who are gender non-conformist. Binary gender associations of male and female are a social construct. They have been created by people, but their existence has become so ingrained that – even from the moment unborn babies have their sex identified during a pregnancy scan – we are gendered. So why do people conform to these made-up rules?

Michel Foucault, a famous French philosopher, was very interested in power structures in society that regulate human behaviours. Having researched and published books on the criminal justice system, Foucault also considered the social structures of sexuality because of his own self-identification as a gay man. He experienced first-hand the social constraints around homosexuality – such as public displays of affection, non-legal recognition of same-sex relationships, and the association of homosexuality as immoral or a sin. Foucault's discussion of 'the panopticon' helps us see why we behave in many of the ways we do (Foucault 1977). The panopticon is a prison with a tower in the centre in which guards are able to have uninterrupted sight of each prisoner. Given that each prisoner knows that they are watched and constantly under surveillance, they begin to regulate their own behaviour. Outside of prison situations, we see how we are constantly under scrutiny in similar ways. Many people dress according to social expectations, and they behave in ways traditionally associated with masculinity or femininity. These social rules and expectations put pressure on people to conform, to self-regulate, to self-scrutinise and to self-judge, and people seek to avoid breaking these codes for fear of criticism from other people. According to Butler, gender becomes 'a stylised repetition of acts' (1988: 519). Following on from de Beauvoir's idea that 'one is not born, but, rather, *becomes* a woman' (2009), gender is stylised through the body. Gestures, movements, and mannerisms all give the 'performativity' of a gender. As with all performances, there are many rehearsals that go on behind the scenes before the final product is showcased. In a similar way, gender performativity is realised through multiple rehearsals, or repetitions. Each individual performance is *temporary*. What gives gender the illusion of being a *permanent* identity is that it is performed by multiple bodies across time and space, and these bodies repeat the performance. Therefore, people think of gender as fixed (and aligned with biological sex), because of these multiple and incessant performativities and repetitions. To go against such expectations is to be judged non-normative and that carries with it certain social consequences, including emotional, psychological and physical violence experienced through transphobia, homophobia, and biphobia.

For those interested in drag, this concise social history of gender normativity is one that has shaped people's self-understanding through the performance art. Through theory, the work of academics has provided us with both language and tools to enable us to understand our own identities, experiences, as well as to que(e)ry the power structures that police the rules of gender in the contemporary world. Butler places drag at the centre of gender theory in its role as a disruptive marker, as she states, 'Drag is an example that is meant to establish that "reality" is not as fixed as we generally assume it to be' (1990: xxv). In her introduction to *Gender Trouble*, Butler sets out a provocation, asking the reader 'is drag the imitation of gender?' (1990: xxxi). Butler draws on Esther Newton's *Mother Camp* (1972), an anthropological study with American drag queens. Here, Butler notes that drag does two things: it disrupts binary gender, and it disrupts the idea that gender has an essential, original truth. Drag therefore playfully mixes and messes with normative expectations of gender.

Thus, drag is queer art! Rather, then, than being an 'imitation' of gender, drag is more aptly described as a destabilisation of gender. Through subversion and parody, fixed gender categories and normative social expectations about gender are disrupted and destabilised. Indeed, this idea about the social construction of gender reveals that the notion of 'female impersonation' or 'male impersonation' that was historically used to describe drag cabaret is wrong. Quite simply, no such pre-existing blue-print of male or female behaviours existed in the first place that could be impersonated! Yet, as we have seen in Chapter 1, these dominant ideas are often used to detail and describe drag. What is being impersonated, and indeed parodied, is the socially constructed illusion of masculine and feminine.

Butler's ideas about the subversion of continue to stir discussions about gender today. Gill Jagger comments how 'her attempt to explain it … through the example of drag, has probably raised more questions that it has solved' (2008: 35). While the disruption and queering of gender has been transformative for many non-binary and genderqueer people, the idea of biological sex remains important to gender critical feminists who reject the notion that sex can be reassigned.

In a direct reference to drag culture, Butler references the iconic film *Paris is Burning* (see Chapter 3), and she notes how the documentary 'made clear drag is not unproblematically subversive' in itself (Butler 1993: 231). Butler notes how drag has the potential to be subversive, but this is dependent on context and reception. If drag is a parody of gender, an exaggeration, a sending up of gender with the intention of comic effect, then the dominant ideas we associate with masculine and feminine are destabilised. They may not be fully displaced, but their neat order is clearly disrupted through drag. In seeking to address this idea of whether drag is always intentionally and purposefully subversive to social norms, Ash Kayte Stokoe sets out clearly that drag can challenge, destabilise, subvert normative powerful systems, but they remind us that this is quite a tall order to ask of drag artists and performers:

It is unrealistic to expect that the art and lives of drag performers and/or of trans people constantly challenge oppressive ideas and systems. To do so is to hold them to a higher standard that gender conventional, cisgender artists, actors and musicians.

(Stokoe 2020a: 17)

THE IMPOSSIBILITY OF DEFINING QUEER

In addition to its use as an identity marker and an academic area of inquiry, queer also has a third usage that can be traced back to its original use as 'odd' or 'strange'. In its continual disruption and displacement of normative ideas and ideals, queer frames itself in antagonistic opposition to the status quo. Because of this, then, queer becomes unfixed and undefinable. Queer must resist closed definitions, because that would result in it being fixed and definable! Queer is a gate-crasher and exposer of power and inequalities; it must remain elusive and uncertain. A clear way to frame this is as follows:

The minute you say 'queer' you are necessarily calling into question exactly what you mean when you say it. There is always an implicit question about what constitutes 'queerness' that attends the minute you say the word.

(Harper, White, & Cerullo 1993: 30)

Defining 'queer' is a futile, pointless task that does not create meaning but, instead, limits and normalises it. Annamarie Jagose says how queer cannot have 'a consistent set of characteristics' (1996: 96). In very similar terms, as we have seen, drag cannot be easily defined and its frame of references is constantly dynamic and shape-shifting. Accordingly, drag is an excellent example of queer theory in practice; it is embodied, lived, unique, individualised, creative, powerful, political. It is a totally original and evolving creation.

There is an almost tension between these two uses, as 'queer' has been used as a catch-all umbrella term for the LGBTQ+ spectrum of identities, as well as a term that subverts identity categorisation. Here, we witness a certain paradox where 'queer' is used as a marker of identity and as an escape artist from identity! So, queer as identity – used to describe LGBTQ+ people – contrasts with its use as a theory and practice, in which the strai(gh)t-jackets of identity ought not to be worn. This tension around definitions of 'queer' can be eased a little if we see queer as a *doing*, rather than a *being*. Chris Greenough reminds us that 'instead of looking at what queer *is* it is better to look at what queer *does*' (2019: 26). 'Queer' is broader than its use to describe non-heterosexual sexualities or non-binary genders, even though its popular use today may be in relation to such identities. In fact, we can trace a much broader definition back to the 1990s, as David Halperin states how 'queer' is more than sexuality:

> [Queer is] ... whatever is at odds with the normal, the legitimate, the dominant. 'Queer' ... demarcates not a positivity but a positionality vis-à-vis the normative – a positionality that is not restricted to lesbians and gay men.
>
> (Halperin 1995: 62)

The call to drag up and disrupt what has been established and what exercises power and control over others has been the catalyst of queer theory. As we shall see in the next section, queer theory's persistent disruption and deconstruction of normative ideas and ideals must insist on intersectional approaches.

INTERSECTIONALITY

Intersectionality is a theoretical framework for understanding how aspects of one's social and political identities (for example, gender, race, class, sexuality, disability, etc.) might combine to create unique modes of discrimination. While it may appear to be a contemporary framework, key thinking by feminist and womanist activists and academics have often shone light on how multiple marginalisation is experienced. Kimberlé Crenshaw (1991) coined the term 'intersectionality' to explore how race and gender intersect to shape Black women's experiences of employment. Crenshaw was concerned with how race and gender had tended to be considered as separate, exclusive or separable identities. Tracing these categories to their intersections exposed how the most marginalised people in society fall under multiple minority groups, and therefore experience multiple systems of oppression.

Crenshaw sets out the three key dimensions: (1) structural intersectionality (how individual experiences in society are different depending on your identity categories); (2) political intersectionality (how social movements paradoxically further marginalise other individuals or groups); and (3) representational intersectionality (the interrogation of cultural representations and constructions of identity categories). Crenshaw's exposé of intersectionality was not solely about race and gender, as she states, 'the concept can and should be expanded by factoring in issues such as class, sexual orientation, age and color' (Crenshaw 1991: 1245).

Intersectionality shows how systems of oppression and discrimination are multiple. Put in very clear terms, intersectionality is concerned with how an individual may be marginalised because of one identity characteristic, but their marginalisation is further compounded when one considers other identity characteristics they have. The purpose of intersectionality as a theory is to identify how overlapping categories of identity impact upon individuals and institutions. Therefore, intersectionality takes these dynamics into account when working to promote social and political equity. In drag performances, elements of misogyny, ageism, heterophobia, biphobia, transphobia, homophobia, disability discrimination, racism and other forms of prejudice-based jibes or 'jokes' have worked their way into live shows in order to shock and attempt to elicit a cheap laugh. Increasingly, though, the time is up on the failure to acknowledge intersectionality, and such prejudice and discrimination no longer shocks; it simply offends.

Gender activism often draws pushback or negative perceptions of those who call out injustices. In her book *Living A Feminist Life* (2017), Sara Ahmed describes the role of the feminist 'killjoy', as she states, 'the figure of the killjoy comes up whenever there are difficulties to bring up' (Ahmed 2017: 267). The killjoy speaks out, and there are risks in doing so, including to life. For Ahmed, speaking out is vital, as silence reproduces injustices and violence. Ahmed reminds us, 'Silence about violence is violence' (2017: 260–261).

One of Ahmed's principles is 'I am not willing to laugh at jokes designed to cause offense' (2017: 261), and this is a mantra many drag audiences can learn from. Humour and laughter are both key components of 'joy', yet their use, function and impact cannot escape issues of identity and representation. Kareem Khubchandani puts this perfectly in the following example:

> One of the reasons we might consider the stakes of realness in performing Black and Latinx celebrities is because of the burden of representation they often carry. To make fun of white celebrities is to make fun of their specific quirks and foibles – they enjoy the privilege of individuality, however to lampoon Kitt of King, iconic as they are, runs the risk of laughing at Black people more broadly.
> (Khubchandani 2023: 65–66)

There are important and obvious tensions in bringing in Ahmed's pivotal work on killjoy feminism and applying it to drag activism. Two key reasons are: first, the risk of coopting or sidelining feminist struggles with drag, rather than aligning them; and second, the uncomfortable history of misogyny within drag. Killjoy feminism challenges power structures in ways that drag does not always do, especially when performed by cis, white men.

Accordingly, queer, trans, non-binary, disabled, and people of colour drag activists do bring joy as part of a dangerous act of resistance. Drag is complex in how there is no unifying ideology, and it would be romanticising the performance art – and be ultimately inaccurate – to claim all drag is activism. Many forms maintain and operate within oppressive systems through upholding gay male privilege. Ahmed notes how 'there can be joy in killing joy' (2017: 268), and drag as a performance art can go beyond stage spaces to engage with living realties and social issues. The Vixen, for example, has called out racism in drag spaces; and Marsha P. Johnson, who fought for trans rights, embodies principles of killjoy activism. Here, drag is not only an act of joy, but an act of survival. For many, drag also brings joy, rather than kills it. The ideas of 'killjoy' and 'bring-joy' is therefore a binary that depends on an individual's personal beliefs, worldviews, background, history, status, characteristics, education, economic stability, among other issues. More significant than these individual factors, though, is the systemic nature of these issues, including how male, cis, gay privilege has permeated LGBTQ+ spaces, and how drag is perceived in the mainstream. In turn, this is reinforced by capitalism and institutions, such as the mainstream media, corporate sponsorship and representations of drag that are not equitable, diverse or inclusive. For drag artists themselves, sanitised drag performances are more commercially viable than those that avoid political engagement. This is an example of the isolation and resistance of killjoy activists. Most noticeable for drag audiences here is the idea of 'complicit joy', which Ahmed defines as the kind of joy that maintains oppressive systems.

These are important and urgent observations which must be attended to in drag studies and drag cultures, so that all marginalised identities can be brought into intersectional analysis. In the following section on drag practice, we offer an overview of how intersectional critiques can be explored in terms of drag's relationship with misogyny, racism, non-binary identities, and transphobia, as well as discrimination based on disability, body conformity, and class.

DRAG IN PRACTICE

KEY ISSUES

There are necessary overlaps between intersectional theory and key issues relating to lived experiences and drag, given that discussions of intersectionality address the marginalisation of particular identities (gender, race, dis/ability) and structures of oppression. Aside from its well-known cultural function as a performance art and form of entertainment in both queer and mainstream spaces, drag artists have positioned themselves in political and social debates in order to speak out against injustices. The quest for social transformation for LGBTQ+ communities has been punctuated by the presence of drag. Drag is a visible marker of in-your-face queer life that incorporates the humour, parody and politics of gender non-conformity and the range of human sexualities. In this, drag makes visible what is often hidden in mainstream politics.

LGBTQ+ RIGHTS

Before academics got their thinking caps on to develop queer theory, the gay rights movement had begun to oppose oppression and homophobia. The decade of the 1960s was a vibrant period for activism and protest in the Global West, with feminism, civil rights and gay and lesbian rights at the forefront of protests. These events ultimately resulted in changes in law in many countries. The protests were in response to the criminalisation of same-sex activities (note: between two men, not between two women, given the sexism of the law makers!), the persecution of LGBTQ+ people, legal restrictions on relationship recognition, adoption rights, access to healthcare, and homophobia/biphobia/transphobia. These protests were the result of deep internal conflicts people felt because of the dominant norms of a heteronormative society. The impact of being gay, lesbian, bisexual, trans or queer was profoundly felt in terms of emotional and psychological effects. Within the history of homosexuality, we see how to be LGBTQ+ was considered as if it were a psychological disorder and was treated like an illness.

Therefore, to be gay was to be sick. Medical interventions attempted to establish cures for such illnesses, with the aim of transforming 'sick' gay or lesbian people into sane, 'well', heterosexuals. This is similar to so-called 'conversion therapy'. Procedures to 'cure' at this time were very invasive, with lasting physical damage. In some examples, gay men underwent castration and lesbians suffered genital mutilation, while shock treatment and hypnosis were also used in experiments labelled as 'treatments'.

For those who, thankfully, did not undergo treatment, there was a personal and social shame attached to same-sex orientations. Personal shame was turned into collective community pride following pivotal events in 1969. In this year, a landmark event in queer history took place. Located on Christopher Street in Greenwich Village in New York City is a gay bar known as the Stonewall Inn (more commonly referred to as Stonewall). This building has been the host to many gay, lesbian, trans, and drag performers. In the early days it also offered a space to queer youth who were homeless and, to this day, it is an important communal space for socialising and meetings for the LGBTQ+ community. Stonewall was often invaded by the police as a push back towards the criminal gangs, who had invested in the bar since 1966. It was also a way of policing the LGBTQ+ bar patrons. This patrolling was to regulate dress codes and physical activity (and impact on the gangs' invested financial gains). The police often swooped on the bar unexpectedly verifying clientele against arbitrary regulations, as Fitzgerald and Marquez write in their informative text *Legendary Children*:

> people of the same gender were not allowed to dance together, openly flirt with each other, or display any physical desire or affection with each other while on the premises, or in any other public spaces, for that matter. Also strictly illegal: any form of public cross-dressing or dressing in a manner that doesn't conform to social gender expectations.
>
> (Fitzgerald & Marquez 2020: 5)

On the night of 28 June 1969, the habitants of this modest bar brought part of New York City to a standstill. Frustrated and often demoralised by the bullying tactics and queerphobia displayed by the New York City Police Department (NYPD), its occupants pushed back as they were fed up of being persecuted during a raid on this night. One patron – described as 'butch' – had been hit on her head by an officer, and was complaining the handcuffs they placed on her were too tight. The woman's identity has been uncertified, but she is named as Stormé DeLarverie by witnesses and by herself. She looked at the bystanders and shouted, 'why don't you guys do something?!' Riots ensued. The well-known trans activists, Marsha P. Johnson and Silvia Rivera, arrived after the riots began. The Stonewall Riots were a set of demonstrations against oppression – political, legal and social. Their focus included advocacy for freedom of choice and liberation for LGBTQ+ people. The legacy of Stonewall lives on today – just one year later in 1970, the first Pride celebrations began to mark the events. Pride is the plural opposite of shame; it renders visible LGBTQ+ people, their relationships, their communities and their activism. Arguably, the whole point of the Pride events was to counter interior feelings of shame.

As will be seen in this chapter, some forms of drag activism are explicitly intersectional, but there is a risk that race and gender privileges, specifically, are reinforced in drag rather than disrupted. These risks are most palpable in the representation of drag in mainstream spaces, with queens overrepresented in comparison to kings, and the vast majority of queens remain white. Despite all its gender subversion, this highlights the continued gendered inequalities within drag culture.

KINGS AND QUEENS: ROYAL TENSIONS

Jack Halberstam pioneered research into drag kings, particularly in *The Drag King Book* (Volcano & Halberstam 1999) and *Female Masculinity* (Halberstam 1998). Halberstam highlights the impact of drag king performances in challenging traditional gender norms. They examine how drag kings – performers who embody and parody masculinity – offer a powerful critique of hegemonic masculinity while also expanding the understanding of female masculinity. Their analysis situates drag king culture within a broader discussion of gender fluidity, performance, and queer identity. Drag kinging has subversive and transformative potential.

Halberstam (1998) focuses on how activism is embedded in drag king performances masculinity that expose how harmful behaviours are. The performativity of masculinity, according to Halberstam, is bound up with misogyny, racism, and homophobia. In one example, Mo B. Dick performs some of the negative and toxic traits of masculinity, including homophobia and misogyny, as he shows distaste for 'homos' and desire for 'girlies' to audiences in the drag clubs (Halberstam 1998: 30). Here, the performance is not about reinforcing prejudice and discrimination, but parodying them to expose their toxic prevalence in masculine cultures.

In Sweden, research by Lööv (2015) explores how drag kinging is a controversial way of supporting and enacting feminist ideologies and activism. Elian, a drag king in the study, comments on how she is able to behave and perform in ways she would not as a woman. Drag kinging can be a way of highlighting the social constraints and expectations placed on women's bodies. It raises consciousness about gender politics, regulation and oppression through personal experiences. Lööv draws a helpful distinction between the two theoretical approaches on drag: Butler's theoretical notion of performativity and Ahmed's focus on living experiences, as they note 'Butler privileges seeing, while Ahmed privileges doing' (Lööv 2015: 107). Importantly, the setting of the drag performances moves from 'safer' spaces, such as clubs, to public, 'heterosexualised' spaces, which offers the art educational and subversive possibilities (2015: 113).

Drag kings do drag differently, according to Lisbeth Berbary and Corey Johnson's study (2016). Their research details drag kings' reflections on their art and identifies four key components through narrative interviews with drag kings: (1) being genderqueer, (2) all gender as performance, (3) misogyny across drag, and (4) drag as activism. Their participants state:

> But there are some of us who do drag differently. We make drag political. We ask what stories we want to tell about … political systems, war, family issues, alcoholism?
>
> (Berbary & Johnson 2016: 311)

The authors identify one key inequity, noting that there has been a dominant focus on drag queens rather than drag kings. This highlights the traditional gender roles and everyday sexism exists in drag too:

> A woman dressed as a man is a tomboy, mostly ignored. But a man dressed as a woman? A body with make-up, high heels, long hair … well 'she' is a spectacle. A big deal! Deserving of attention. Anyone transforming into a beautiful women will be slathered with compliments. Dress like a guy, and not one … And that's frustrating. And the misogyny we put up with. Drag queen, big-barbies with their hyper-glamorized version of femininity – well some of them still hold onto their high level of privilege and entitlement that comes from being a man. Dress like a women, but you can't kick out the male privilege in them!
>
> (Berbary & Johnson 2016: 311)

Kerryn Drysdale sums up the paradoxes between mainstream and non-normative drag cultures well in her research on drag king cultures specifically. She writes how 'drag cultures, it would seem, are often capable of resilience in their celebration of non-normative culture, while simultaneously allowing for self-reflection in moments of internal political contradictions' (Drysdale 2019: 188). This contradiction should not be understood in binary terms 'either/or': either mainstream or subcultures; kings versus queens. To understand concepts in binary terms is very normative! Therefore, drag cultures can be understood as 'both/and'. Drag can be both celebratory and problematic, and all the spaces in between.

DRAG AND MISOGYNY

The concise survey of the relationship between drag kings and queens noted above exposes some of the controversial and contentious problems found in drag cultures. A further complexity in the relationship between drag and misogyny is found in problematic and discriminatory drag histories. Unfortunately, some of these persist to the present day. In *RuPaul's Drag Race* season six, Gia Gunn enters the workshop, describing herself as 'a fishy queen'. The term was originally used to describe drag queens who sought to present in ways that convince audiences they are feminine, rather than exaggerating aspects of femininity; the term relates to a derogatory description of female genitalia. The term 'f*shy', despite its widespread usage on previous seasons of the show, has been adopted in drag cultures without attention being paid to its offensive etymology. The term is entirely misogynistic, and it has rightfully been debated, critiqued and largely eliminated in public forums, including on social media. The use of the term can be traced to a complex and uncomfortable history of gay male misogyny, where derogatory comments about women's genitalia have formed the basis of jokes. Jokes that deride women or their bodies are, without question, a form of misogyny that needs calling out and eradicating. Drag is constantly evolving, just like language is, and it is right that such concerns are voiced in order to push back against the status quo.

Drag queens have been at the receiving end of some forms of feminist critique. Assigned male at birth, they, arguably, benefit from patriarchal privileges. The exaggeration of the female body, through parody and sexualisation in terms of breasts and hips, becomes problematic when it is considered through a male-oriented view of women. Indeed, AFAB (assigned female at birth) queens offer a further gender distinction that points to transmisogyny in some parts of drag subcultures. Often named 'bioqueens' or 'faux queens', both of these terms have since become controversial as they are transphobic in terms of conflating and prioritising biological sex with gender, and the terms imply that a trans woman who performs as a drag queen is not female.

Drag has a difficult and controversial relationship with misogyny. Many hypermasculine gay men and communities seek to disassociate themselves from camp and feminisation, and there has been a rejection of drag queen performances in a number of gay subcultures. In the 1980s and 1990s, critiques against drag queens came to the fore by lesbian feminists, who sought to align drag with misogyny. Marilyn Frye (1983) writes about the place of misogyny in gay subculture, where the politics of lesbian feminists cannot align with gay culture because male privilege still flexes its muscles. Janice Raymond builds on these concerns, as she notes:

> Cross dressers, drag queens, and heterosexual transvestites – who clandestinely parade around in ultrafeminine dress while often retaining their public personas as straight, white, male conservative pillars of the community – depend upon a certain mimicry of women's persons, roles, status, and dress. That some men may find gender relief, sexual pleasure, and/or stardom and financial profit in this mimicry does nothing to challenge the political power of the normative, dominant, powerful class of men that the male gender bender still belongs to.
>
> (Raymond 1994: xxviii)

Raymond is, of course, using terminology that was considered current at the time but has become outdated in light of today's more nuanced understandings of gender and sexuality. There is no longer the idea that drag is a form of transsexualism or cross-dressing done by straight men for sexual kicks; it is an art form. Some of these misunderstandings possibly arise from its subcultural form, before it became mainstream, and/or its fetishisation in literature such as *Female Mimics* (see Chapter 1). As it may have been subcultural and, for the majority, limited to queer spaces in times before the digital age, there were many misunderstandings of the purpose and impact of drag performance.

Additionally, this critique relies on a confusion between the two terms: sex and gender, and such a conflation leads to the wrong conclusion that gender is fixed, stable, and biological, rather than performative (see earlier). Indeed, in contemporary views, we note how the same critiques have reemerged in transphobia and trans-misogyny. One of the respondents to Raymond's ideology at the time was Judith Butler, who counter-critiques these arguments in the following way:

> The problem with the analysis of drag as only misogyny is, of course, that it figures male-to-female transsexuality, cross-dressing,

and drag as male homosexual activities – which they are not always – and it further diagnoses male homosexuality as rooted in misogyny.

(Butler 1999: 339–340)

Butler observes how such debates result in a zero-sum game:

According to these views, drag is nothing but the displacement and appropriation of 'women', and hence fundamentally based on misogyny, a hatred of women; and lesbianism is nothing but the displacement and appropriation of men, and so fundamentally a matter of hating men – misandry.

(Butler 1999: 340)

Nonetheless, the wider debates do shed light on how gay men do benefit from male privilege, despite their own marginalised masculinities. A further issue raised by these discussions is that they destabilise the assumed allegiances and allyship of the LGBTQ+ community. The abbreviation LGBTQ+ is sometimes used universally, yet each identity category has its own political aims, its own injustices, and its own identity-based activism.

DRAG AND RACISM

Drag Race has achieved popular appeal by trafficking in well-worn racist and transphobic tropes.

(Horowitz 2020: 103)

Horowitz's point is astutely accurate; drag has a problematic history with racism. Contemporary criticism and analysis of drag should absolutely explore and interrogate such intersectional issues. The privilege of whiteness and the Western hegemony in drag representation remain the dominant lens by which drag is viewed. As noted in the introduction, Kareem Khubchandani's book *Decolonize Drag* (2023), is essential reading for those seeking to dismantle systemic portrayals of drag. Khubchandani's argument is 'how urgently we need a decolonized drag to break, bust, shatter, unsettle and undo the binary structures put in place by Euro-American empires' (Khubchandani 2023: 7). In terms of activism specifically, the yardstick of drag is problematic because of its racial dominance. Khubchandani illustrates how 'the cultural, artistic, and activist practice that we know as drag has come to be measured through global whiteness' (2023: 28). As well as disrupting gender, there are examples where drag challenges discrimination in relation to race/ethnicity, religion, dis/ability and misogyny.

In another excellent example of critique into how drag intersects with race, Ash Kayte Stokoe, explores bell hooks' analysis of Harlem drag ball subcultures and *Paris Is Burning* (see Stokoe 2020a). hooks argues how 'colonized black people ... worship at the throne of whiteness, even when such worship demands that we live in perpetual self-hate, steal, lie, go hungry, and even die in its pursuit' (hooks 1992: 149). For hooks, a performance of whiteness by queens of colour is inherently motivated by internalised racism. Stokoe illuminates how, according to hooks, heterosexual Black men in drag draw on 'racist, colonial attitudes to black masculinity, seeking to render this masculinity funny and harmless by deploying homophobia and misogyny' (Stokoe 2020a: 56).

A similar observation is noted by Rusty Barrett, whose study of language used by African-American drag queens (Barrett 1998) use a 'white woman' style of speech in order to communicate in ways deemed more fitting for a 'lady'. Cultural associations with the term 'lady' include privileged identity categories such as middle or upper class and heterosexual. Barrett talks about how this use of language is stereotypical, rather than really reflecting language used by a particular group, and ultimately the privilege of whiteness indicates a move away from language used by Black people. In terms of language use, elsewhere, Ash Kayte Stokoe discusses representations of ethnicity and prejudice against non-native speakers of English in *RuPaul's Drag Race* (Stokoe 2020b).

Sabrina Strings and Long T. Bui (2014) examine the absence of intersecting identity markers of gender and race in the third season of *RuPaul's Drag Race*. They note how racial stereotypes are prevalent during the series, as they state the following:

> This overt raceing became problematic for the contestants in two ways. First, coming from marginalized groups in society, the queens were sensitive to ethnic (mis)appropriation. Thus, they became defensive when cast members donned racial personas,

viewing these performances as offensive forms of mockery or minstrelsy. Second, black and brown cast members were more often required to perform stereotypical racial identities. RuPaul would refer to such performances as giving 'personality'.

(Strings & Bui 2014: 824)

Wrongly linking racial stereotypes with 'personality' means that white privilege goes unmarked and unnoticed. The troubling conclusion from Strings and Bui is that drag subculture remains largely divided by race, gender and class. Indeed, to use the term 'drag subculture' would be to conceive of drag as one distinct counter-cultural group, and therefore the plural term 'subcultures' is more fitting, as this points to the existence of varied groups with different shared identity categories.

Throughout history, drag performers have spoken out against racial injustice and discrimination, and this has been a hallmark of drag and trans activism, with pioneering figures such as Silvia Rivera and Marsha P. Johnson noted previously. Drag has a place in terms of activism and protest in relation to the Black Lives Matter (BLM) movement. BLM is focussed on addressing racism and racially motivated violence, including police persecution of Black people. The first use of the hashtag #BlackLivesMatter was in 2013, following the acquittal of George Zimmerman for second degree murder after he killed a 17-year-old Black teenager, Trayvon Martin. This led to the national prominence of BLM in protests in New York City. It was in 2020 that the movement gained international attention, during the global Covid pandemic. A Minneapolis police officer, Derek Chauvin, murdered George Floyd, a 46-year-old Black man, by kneeling on his neck for over nine minutes. Floyd complained he could not breathe and died under the restraint. Chauvin pleaded guilty, and was sentenced to just under 23 years in prison. Videos of the incident appeared across social media and news outlets, and all officers involved were fired.

Given the events that took place in New York, it is unsurprising that drag queens from *RuPaul's Drag Race* have used their platforms to advocate for BLM and speak out against racial injustice. Some of the most vocal activists include season eight winner Bob the Drag Queen, who co-founded the Black Queer Town Hall alongside season nine contestant Peppermint, who has become a trans icon. The aim of the Black Queer Town Hall is community focussed, uplifting Black people and amplifying Black voices. Peppermint's activism extends beyond just drag – she works directly with groups like the Marsha P. Johnson Institute (https://marshap.org) and the Okra Project (www.theokraproject.com), which focus on supporting Black trans individuals. The Marsha P. Johnson Institute was founded as a response to the murders of Black trans women and women of colour, yet it directly addresses social justice issues, namely racial, gender, and reproductive justice, as well as gun violence. The Okra Project provides mutual aid for Black trans people. Similarly, season ten standout The Vixen has never shied away from difficult conversations about racism, both within the drag world and beyond. Frustrated with the lack of representation, she created *Black Girl Magic*, a show that celebrates Black queens and ensures they have the spotlight they deserve.

RuPaul's Drag Race's very first winner, BeBe Zahara Benet, continues to push for change. As one of the most visible African queens in mainstream drag, she has long fought for better representation of Black and African LGBTQ+ people in entertainment. Following a similar path, a number of other Black queens are at the forefront of highlighting racism within society and culture. For example, *All Stars* season five winner Shea Couleé has not only marched in protests but also consistently donated to Black-led organisations, using her success to give back to the community. Season thirteen winner, Symone, infuses her performances with powerful imagery, often referencing Black history and the ongoing fight against police brutality. For example, in season thirteen, Symone showcased a 'Say Their Names' runway look, honouring victims of police violence. These examples are not exhaustive and offer just a snapshot of the important commitment to social justice through anti-racism education and dismantling systemic racism through exposure. That said, RuPaul herself has been critiqued for her expensive forms of drag, in which 'whiteness' equates to the Glamazon, as Khubchandani states:

> As a Black performer in racist nightlife and media culture of the eighties, she leans on whiteness as a means of finding mobility. However, as her career skyrockets, she does little to unsettle or question white aesthetics. Rather, she becomes the arbiter of perfection, professionalism, conformity, and even the gender binary.
>
> (Khubchandani 2023: 88)

It has been notable that RuPaul was silent on BLM issues (Reynolds 2020), though the editorial choices from werkroom scenes did showcase discussions between the contestants about their activism (RuPaul's Drag Race 2021). Many drag performers are involved in and approach activism in their own ways, whether through protests, performances, fundraising, or creating safe spaces.

While the platform of *RuPaul's Drag Race* allowed heightened visibility to the queens participating in BLM protests and activism in the USA, the drag king community has often been active in addressing racism (see Halberstam 1998). *Kings of the World* was a monthly drag king show streamed through American live-streaming services. The shows were co-produced by Los Angeles drag kings, Mo B. Dick, Pelvis Breastly and Johnny Gentleman. The third show in June 2020 was postponed and dedicated to the memory of George Floyd and the entire cast of kings performing in the show was Black (Momma's Boyz Drag Kings 2020).

Music has also been an activist outlet for drag performers. Drag King Alex U. Inn is an activist and community leader in San Francisco (USA), as well as co-founder of the hip hop drag king group, Momma's Boyz. He released the song *Glory* in response to BLM events, which highlights racial injustice and heightened racism. Inn's message is that 'the biggest weapon is to stay peaceful' while being committed to standing up to change. Peaceful does not mean silent or inactive; it points to a very firm physical presence and message that denounces violence in all forms.

While racism continues to shape drag cultures, another pressing issue is the persistent reinforcement of binary gender norms within drag communities, often leading to the marginalisation of non-binary and trans identities.

DRAG, NON-BINARY IDENTITIES, AND TRANSPHOBIA

Drag is often considered to be the exaggeration and parody of gender – with hyper-masculinities and hyper-femininities forming part of what becomes instantly recognisable as drag. Interestingly, despite the significant role of drag in LGBTQ+ histories and the role of queer theory discussed above, the interpretation of drag seems shockingly to reinforce binary gender in some representations. Drag queens and drag kings seem to reinforce normative stereotypes of gender binaries, with queening dominating discussions of drag through its popularity in the mainstream media. While drag includes presentations from transgender, non-binary, or genderqueer people who disrupt gender, the tendency to view drag as 'opposite sex' performance is still prominent. Ash Kayte Stokoe puts this neatly:

> As some iconic 'male impersonators' and 'female impersonators' performed gender which differed from their own, certain theorists have used their examples as a basis for generalization and incorrectly assumed that drag *necessarily* involves performing as 'the opposite sex'.
>
> (Stokoe 2020a: 2)

To think of drag in 'opposite sex' performances limits drag and queerness. In Chapter One, we trace the evolution of drag and its earlier labels such as 'female impersonation' or 'male impersonation', which, although popular at the time and in the documentation of histories, are now outdated. Drag is only ever read with contemporary eyes, and therefore the social, cultural and political locations in which it is performed form part of its reception as a performance art.

The notion of 'opposite sex' drag has been perpetuated by drag in the mainstream media. Jorge González and Kameron Cavazos (2016) make an interesting observation about the popular TV series *RuPaul's Drag Race*, noting how the mini-challenges in earlier seasons of the show include wet t-shirt competitions, the use of breast and hip padding, and how masculine or genderqueer presentations in earlier series of the show were derided by the judges, who insisted on reading and valorising 'femininity'. González and Cavazos note how this actually reinforces the binaries of gender and sexuality. They explain the consequences for those who do not perform according to these boundaries, stating 'it becomes clear that genderqueer drag queens and those who wish to portray anything more than a binary expression of heteronormative gender are not valued nor are they successful on the show' (González & Cavazos 2016: 663).

It is ironic, therefore, that an art form whose simple existence is to disrupt gender, actually begins to reinforce cisnormativity and gender binaries! Katie Horowitz invokes Lisa Duggan's concept of 'homonormativity' to explain transphobia in drag (Horowitz 2020). Homonormativity is the assimilation of LGB people with heterosexual culture, so that heterosexual rules and structures are privileged in terms of dating, relationships, appearances, family structures, consumerism, and so on. Homonormativity can be seen in LGB rights for same-sex marriage, parenting and adoption, while trans people's rights to safety are not assured. This reveals a tension in the acronym LGBTQ+, where each letter has its own agenda and business, and, as homonormativity exposes, one group does not always advocate or support another. Horowitz discusses how *Drag Race* embodies the norm of homonormativity, and states, 'Nowhere is *Drag Race*'s appeal to that norm clearer than in its exclusion of transfemininity' (Horowitz 2020: 103). Fenton Litwiller makes this point in much starker and sobering terms, noting how drag queens may be celebrated in queer communities, but may not have to confront the microaggressions and daily violence that trans women experience. In terms of how drag reinforces gender binaries rather than subverting them, Litwiller notes how limiting drag to 'opposite sex' definitions becomes 'an act of cisgender privilege and transgender exclusion rather than just a mockery of the everyday gender framework' (Litwiller 2020: 608).

DRAG AND DISABILITY

Ableism follows the pattern of other '-isms' that denote prejudice (for example, sexism, racism, classism). Ableism is the discrimination and social prejudice against disabled people that invokes the concept of 'normality'. Ableism is rooted in the assumption that disabled people require 'fixing' through medical interventions, and defines (and attempts to limit) people by their disability. Representations of people with physical disabilities in drag performances have been extremely rare, but of course not all disabilities are visible.

Representations of disabilities on *RuPaul's Drag Race* have been few and far between. In series eleven, Yvie Oddly disclosed she had hypermobility Ehlers-Danlos syndrome – a condition where loose, unstable joints may dislocate easily, or cause joint pain. It was not until episode six that Oddly revealed her condition, and stated that 'I didn't want to make it clear that I had any sort of weakness holding me back … It's not because I'm ashamed of it, but there is this tendency of people to kind of write off or discredit invisible disability' (Ehlers Danlos Society 2019). Oddly went on to snatch the crown, and was named winner of the season. In season thirteen, Tamisha Iman reveals how she was due to appear on season twelve but had received a cancer diagnosis. Throughout the weekly challenges, she did not initially disclose to the other contestants that she had an ostomy bag. In season two of *RuPaul's Drag Race UK*, Ginny Lemon revealed they have fibromyalgia and therefore could not wear heeled shoes; Lemon subsequently quit the show. Critiques of disability discrimination have also been raised where contestants have misused walking aids or medical equipment in their looks, such as season ten where the queens used wheelchairs to move down the catwalk runway as they were dressed as mermaids.

The situations described above, including where contestants chose to withhold their conditions until they were no longer able to hide them through physical pain, bear testament to the ableism at play in society broadly, and in queer and drag cultures specifically. Happily, one counter narrative to this embraces more positive portrayals of drag, where ableism is slayed. Drag Syndrome is the world's first drag troupe featuring drag performers with Down syndrome (see www.dragsyndrome.com). The company ruptures the ableist lenses that have been at play in drag performance and actively challenges hegemonic representations of drag (see Edward & Farrier 2020). Drag must continue to rupture its own expectations, in line with its continuous queer activism in order to celebrate diversity and difference.

Activist joy can be found in the creation of accessible drag spaces. In their chapter on 'Drag, Access and Queer Crip Joy as an Act of Resistance', Amelia Lander-Cavallo and Al Lander-Cavallo (2025) explore how 'queer crip joy' becomes an act of resistance in drag, expanding the idea on what drag is and does as a political art. Amelia's drag practice is as Tito Bone, 'your average blind non-binary bisexual drag king' (2025: xii). They use the word 'crip' as an insult reclaimed, in many ways similar to how 'queer' has been reclaimed over time: from a slur to an activist marker of identity. Stripping language from the power of its discriminatory uses, the reclamation of terms such as 'crip' and 'queer' show activist potential. Using such terms calls out the oppressor and exclusionary practices.

Tito's drag performance centres accessibility as part of inclusive performance practices, including the use of audio description and mobility accommodations as fundamental to performance rather than an afterthought:

> It is rare for a drag show to have any kind of access embedded into it. In our experience this is because there aren't resources available to put access into place, because people are unaware of what access is needed or, in some of the worst cases, people in charge of drag shows and spaces don't have any impetus to engage with accessibility.
>
> (Lander-Cavallo & Lander-Cavallo 2025: 130)

When considering representation in relation to drag cultures, it is not only the performers and artists who form part of this reflection, diverse audiences are paramount to the project of inclusion, too. Here, care, access, wellbeing and safety become the criteria for drag performances, and, in turn, these build new spaces for joy and self-expression. The authors reject tokenism and 'inspiration porn', arguing that disabled drag performers should not be framed as exceptional or overcoming their disabilities.

Most significantly, Lander-Cavallo and Lander-Cavallo highlight how ableism has functioned in queer spaces for far too long. Not only this, but the inclusion agenda expands the abundance and creativity in drag performance. While drag is highly visual, relying on make-up, costumes, performances, lip-synced and dance, the use of audio description addresses urgent interventions in relation to inclusive practices, but also create new opportunities for storytelling and audience engagement. These innovations speak back to mainstream drag cultures and its systemic ableist practices that form barriers to inclusion.

DRAG AND BODY CONFORMITY

In-your-face visibility is part of drag performance, where radical fashions, make-up, prosthetics, wigs, shoes, clothing, accessories all form part of a bold aesthetic. One area of critical scholarship that seeks to challenge body conformity is fat studies, a field of inquiry that seeks to embrace body positivity and acceptance for people of all sizes. Fat studies challenges the negative perceptions around fat bodies in society.

Through intersectional approaches that examine drag and fatness, we see an invisible yet powerful tightrope that balances two positions: one in which a performer articulates their self-love for their shape and size, and another that explores how their life stories are punctuated with episodes in which they had to resist sizeism and fatphobia. The medical model of fatness, and its erroneous connotations with laziness, greed, weakness, and unattractiveness, holds a legacy in drag subcultures where fatness is still taboo. This is equally reflected in gay gym cultures. While larger men have been embraced in gay subcultures as 'bears', plus size drag still poses a problem in terms of aesthetics, and therefore fat drag performers seemingly have to overcompensate for a perceived lack of beauty with comedy.

Indeed, while plus size queens have participated in *RuPaul's Drag Race* as contestants, it was only in series two of *RuPaul's Drag Race UK* that a plus-size queen, Lawrence Channey, was crowned winner. Ami Pomerantz (2017) offers a critical examination of big girls in *RuPaul's Drag Race*, and observes how tokenism is often at play in the selection of drag performers for the show. Pomerantz states 'A casting policy that is careful to include at least one (token) fat queen every season is so transparent that all the contestants recognize it. This causes fat queens to feel that they have to justify being selected to [*RuPaul's Drag Race*] for reasons *other* than being the token fat queen' (Pomerantz 2017: 110, emphasis ours).

In her work on fat activism, Charlotte Cooper highlights the relationship between queer and activism, exposing how queer identities can and should be activist ones. She laments how, regrettably, the activist potential of queer has been limited:

Queer rhymes with sneer and has an anti–normative, anti–assimilationist and punk streak to it. Yet in some circles queer contradicts this and has also become a synonym for a restrictive kind of gay identities, that of young, able-bodied, white, affluent, conformist, urban men. This paradox illustrates the slippery nature of queer and the difficulty, or rather inappropriateness, of trying to pin it down.

(Cooper 2016: 192)

Cooper's emphasis on this tension shows the use of the term 'queer' as a fixed, limiting and restrictive identity category is problematic when co-opted to describe privileged characteristics. As noted earlier, queer needs to remain unstable and contested to retain its potency.

DRAG AND CLASS

In this section, consideration of drag against various diverse inter-sectional identities has, thus far, demonstrated how drag is not simply a disruptor of gender, but it intersects and must interrogate other aspects of identity such as race, ability, body size, and so on. One invisible marker that exists in drag culture is class. In socio-economic terms, the drag industry can be quite the money-maker. In her landmark essay 'Notes on Camp' (first published in 1964), Susan Sontag describes how 'the hallmark of camp is the spirit of extravagance. Camp is a woman walking around in a dress made of three million feathers' (Sontag 1983: 112). Therefore, as camp and drag have historically been intertwined, the relationship between drag and wealth merits further attention and closer critical exami-nation in academic studies than it has received to date. Costumery, accessories, and merchandise all cost significant amounts of money that are sourced through specialist outlets. The judgement on one's aesthetic as 'haute couture' or as 'cheap' is simply a judgement of how much money a performer has been able to invest into their look. Drag intersects with class in dynamic ways which still often privileges people with wealth.

Irreverent queer plus-size drag comes in no bolder form than Divine, whose iconic performance in John Waters's *Hairspray* (1988) as the mother of Tracy Turnblad disrupted both gender and body norms and their dominant representations on screen. Divine's per-formances, as Ragan Rhyne argues (2004), expose how codes of femininity are specifically dependent on class codes. In fact, drag is totally decentred through Divine, according to Rhyne:

> Fat, as a class marker, comes to be a primary code through which Divine's drag performance denaturalizes the whiteness implicit in normative femininity. In fact, this camp project of reassigning

value to the valueless is achieved primarily through the performance of whiteness, or of 'white trash' more specifically.

(Rhyne 2004: 190)

Through drag, a performer's socio-economic realities can become
erased or blurred, and it is rare that such a representation favours
performances that reflect working-class cultures. Perhaps it is
acknowledged that many viewers may want to escape some of the
harsh realities that accompany financial hardship, especially due to
increased rates of inflation and cost of living crises. However, such a
line of thinking would seek to explain away issues of representation.
Fundamental to drag is the notion of escapism, of comedy and of
parody, and when drag treads too heavily on sensitive issues such as
poverty and deprivation, the harsh political and material realities of
daily life are made visible.

Mark Edward's *Council House Movie Star* (2012) depicts the off-
stage life of an ageing drag performer, including her vulnerabili-
ties and the bleak realities of poor, urban life in the north-west of
England. The performance is staged, and not a documentary, but it
combines elements from Edward's own working-class upbringing
on a council estate in England during the 1970s and 1980s. The film
is unique in its portrayal of drag in unexpected places (outside of a
club), and this renders the drag performer more vulnerable against
the backdrop of working-class housing and cultures (see Edward
2018 for further discussion).

Beyond individual identities, drag's role as a political tool must be
examined in its activist context. The following section explores how
drag has been mobilised in various forms of advocacy and resistance.

DRAG AND ACTIVISM

CASE STUDIES

This final section offers further exploration of activism in the
form of short case studies related to the following political themes:
LGBTQ+ activism; gender-based violence and #MeToo; religion
and activism; advocacy for sexual health; awareness raising for mental health, and climate change. Of course, the 'basics' nature of this
book means that it is impossible to document all activist activities,
and the concise selection here is based on the significance of the

events in contemporary society and culture. We are aware of limitations in this scope; yet the simple aim is to provide a snapshot of drag's intersections with activism.

LGBTQ+ ACTIVISM

In terms of LGBTQ+ activism, rights, protest, and reform, drag has occupied a visible headlining presence. Tom Fitzgerald and Lorenzo Marquez (2020) detail how drag has been at the forefront of queer life and history. They write, 'Drag queens and kings have been at the center of queer life and present at every single battle and celebration in the past century of queer history. When they weren't the soldiers on the front line, they were the queer fife and drum corps, keeping time and urging the community to continue pressing on' (Fitzgerald & Marquez 2020: 240). Kareem Khubchandani agrees, writing how 'our fabulosity and feathers often make it easy to forget the histories of violence and activism that preceded our shows – laws against cross-dressing, police harassment, protests, vigils and die-ins' (Khubchandani 2023: 15). Rupp et al. see drag king performances as activist, noting how they 'performed in numbers with the intention of challenging their audience not only on issues of gender and sexuality, but race, class, body size, and war, to name a few' (Rupp et al. 2010: 287).

There is a long history of drag activism in relation to LGBTQ+ issues (see Lawson & Lloyd Knight 2019). Readers in the Global West, where certain protections have been legalised for LGBTQ+ people, must not see drag activism solely as a historical event on the journey to secure these rights. There are contemporary battles that still rage on and deserve focus and attention. In terms of rights for LGBTQ+ people, the International Lesbian, Gay, Bisexual, Trans and Intersex Association (www.ilga.org) is an independent organisation that monitors the social and political contexts of LGBTQ+ lives and activism across the globe. They document legislative change across the world that both advances LGBTQ+ rights, and, the worrying trend that sees the reversal of LGBTQ+ rights. The threat against LGBTQ+ rights is a constant battle, even in countries where legal protection is afforded. LGBTQ+ people's lives and identities are constantly a source for 'debate', in many ways heterosexual and cisgender people will never experience. These debates – on various media platforms including television, radio, social media – are a constant microaggression and a daily reminder of the need to continue advocacy and activism. Advancements and even legal protection for LGBTQ+ people do not mean homophobia, biphobia, transphobia and queerphobia have been erased.

Activism does not always take the form of protest. Every individual can be an activist on a micro-level, including discussions with friends and family that challenge perceptions and educate, involvement in local community issues, advocacy and amplification on social media, fundraising and campaigning, voting in elections, among other activities. While the majority of themes in this section do focus on protest and public demonstrations of activism, quotidian acts that serve to change the world one step at a time also deserve credit. Indeed, even as commercialised and mainstream as drag may have become, drag is a political vehicle for the celebrity drag performers and artists who use their platform to speak out and advocate on issues of injustice. For example, Bob the Drag Queen (season eight, *RuPaul's Drag Race*) details how they had been arrested for speaking out on LGBTQ issues, in drag. Bob is activist in fundraising and supporting charity events, as noted previously.

One popular example of political activism was Panti Bliss in the lead-up to Ireland's 2015 vote on marriage equality. In 2014, following a heated media controversy, Bliss gave a moving address, known as the 'Noble Call' at the Abbey Theatre in Dublin (National Museum of Ireland 2014). The speech highlighted the everyday realities, microaggressions, and violence of homophobia experienced by LGBTQ+ people. Subsequently, Bliss became the popular face of the 'Yes' campaign, which encouraged people to vote in favour of marriage equality. Bliss's example shows how activism and advocacy can contribute significantly to contemporary issues. The combination of platform, personal testimony and public performance shaped political change in Ireland, with 62% of voters ultimately backing same-sex marriage.

The synergy of drag and activism makes a perfect pairing as drag serves to upset the status quo. Given its constant agenda of disrupting norms, drag's ability to overturn the assumed stability of policy, practices and law upsets the existing state of affairs, especially regarding social and political issues. For all its campness and performativity, through its activism, drag is a serious form, a serious art, a catalyst for change.

GENDER-BASED VIOLENCE AND #METOO

The relationship between misogyny and gender-based violence came to the fore following #MeToo. In 2017, the hashtag phenomenon of #MeToo was extremely popular on social media. It is important to note that the movement did not start there. The #MeToo movement was started by civil rights activist Tarana Burke in 2006, who first used the phrase 'Me Too' on social media to raise consciousness about sexual violence. The #MeToo movement became a platform for people of all genders to share their own experiences of abuse, although in the case of men, it was seen as a sabotage on a space originally created for and designed by women. Bianca Fileborn and Rachel Loney-Howes (2019) note how this prevented other stories being told. In particular, they note how #MeToo seems to represent the experiences of certain victims of sexual assault: young, white, cisgender, heterosexual women. This highlights how the experiences of LGBTQ+ people, sex workers, women of colour, disabled women and women from low socio-economic backgrounds are all neglected in the discussion.

The zeitgeist of #MeToo was evident in popular drag culture, too. In the twelfth season of *RuPaul's Drag Race*, Sherry Pie was disqualified following multiple revelations of sexual misconduct. The season still aired and Pie progressed to the final, but was barred from participation. There were condemnations of the decision to air the series, even though Pie's involvement had been heavily edited out, and the production company explained that it was out of respect for the other queens in the series.

Studies suggest that lesbian, gay, bisexual and trans people experience sexual violence at higher rates than straight people, with around half of trans people experiencing sexual assault at some point in their lives (Benner & Grove 2023). As LGBTQ+ people already face higher rates of stigma, violence (UCLA School of Law Williams Institute 2022), and poverty (Human Rights Campaign n.d.), this marginalisation increases the risk of hate crimes, including sexual violence. While the space of #MeToo may be contested as giving voice to some groups of people, the need for support services to talk about, address, assist, and protect LGBTQ+ people from sexual violence remains an urgent task.

RELIGION AND ACTIVISM

Many global religious traditions take 'conservative' attitudes towards same-sex relations, LGBTQ+ parenting, the recognition and rights of trans people, among other issues. The word 'conservative' is constantly used by the media and groups themselves in a way to politely demarcate how their intention is to uphold traditional family values. In reality, the word serves as a buffer synonym for 'prejudiced' or 'discriminatory', as Greenough has noted elsewhere (2020: 109); it is a manoeuvre the groups themselves would resist. Yet the prejudice is real and must be acknowledged by using the correct terminology to describe queerphobia in all its forms. Many of the religious pronouncements on LGBTQ+ groups deny their existence, designate their identities and relationships as sinful and shameful, and fail to support LGBTQ+ people who have been raised in their traditions. In practice, many of the opponents to drag queer story hour claim to be from Christian groups. (see Chapter 1 on drag panic; Flood 2019). Religion is therefore an important site of controversy and challenge for queer activists, and drag has drawn attention to this hostility and prejudice.

One of the earliest records of a Jewish drag king is through the archives of Pepi Litman (Zylbercweig 1934). Litman was a Yiddish vaudeville singer up until her death in 1930. Growing up in poverty in Galicia, (now in Ukraine), Litman was involved in the expansion of vaudeville theatre in Eastern Europe. Although the term drag king had not been popularised then, Litman certainly was a prototype. Litman dressed as a 'Hasid', a godly Jewish man. Litman kept Jewish law by being kosher and lighting candles on Shabbat even when on the road, and incorporated Jewish culture into her act. Her burial plot was donated by the Jewish Community. It is intriguing how, through this last symbolic act, Pepi's burial demonstrates how her artistry was valued by a Jewish community, and this contrasts sharply with the religious backlash given to other drag artists from their religious groups.

The queer drag nuns the Sisters of Perpetual Indulgence (SPI) first appeared in San Francisco, USA in 1979. As a parody of the nuns who take religious orders in the Roman Catholic Church, the SPI drag up the aesthetic of religious nuns, in a move that speaks back to the homophobic/biphobic pronouncements on LGBTQ+ identities and same-sex relationships of the Catholic Church. The mission of the nuns is 'to promulgate universal joy and to expiate stigmatic guilt'. The SPI are activists involved in charity work, street protest, and performance, and they use religious imagery and iconography to make a satirical jibe against conservative Christian attitudes to LGBTQ+ people. The SPI note how, as real nuns, they are concerned with the spiritual needs of the community that they serve. Although formed in the USA, the SPI have global houses and missions in Australia, Canada, Colombia, across Europe and in Uruguay. Each house is concerned with local issues. SPI do not identify as 'drag queens or kings' per se, rather as 'nun drag'. Melissa Wilcox has been a leading scholar on the identity, organisation, beliefs and practices of the SPI. She refers to their mission as 'serious parody'. In defining this, Wilcox states how '"serious parody" simultaneously critiques and reclaims cultural traditions in the interest of supporting the lives and political objectives of marginalized groups' (Wilcox 2018: 2).

The nuns have been at the forefront of activist events and protest, particularly in the promotion of sexual health education, as seen through their active and prolific campaigns of HIV/AIDS education in New York in the 1980s. The organisation says how they were placed on a list of heretics by the Roman Catholic Church in 1984, following their mock exorcism of Pope John Paul II during his visit to San Francisco. Massive protests were held for the date of the papal visit by civil rights groups. Their demonstration was in direct response to the publication from the Vatican, authored by the later Pope Benedict XVI. The Church's publication noted the following offensive statement against lesbian, gay and bisexual people: 'Although the particular inclination of the homosexual person is not a sin, it is a more or less strong tendency ordered toward an intrinsic moral evil; and thus the inclination itself must be seen as an objective disorder' (Congregation for the Doctrine of Faith 1984). The SPI's work continues, and they are regularly seen at activist protests and in queer spaces.

In Kenya, George Barasa has used his drag status to advocate for LGBTQ+ rights, particularly in support of LGBTQ+ Christian people. In *Kenyan, Christian, Queer* Adriaan van Klinken (2019) details Barasa's story of rejection from his family and community when outed by the Kenyan press, which resulted in mental ill-health and a suicide attempt. Barasa became one of the founding members of Cosmopolitan Affirming Church in Kenya in 2013, and he established the Out in Kenya organisation. He self-describes as follows: 'My name is George Barasa. Or Joji Baro. I am 22 years old. I was born in Nairobi and brought up in Bungoma. I am a Gospel artist. I am Gay. I am HIV/AIDS positive. I am an activist. And I am a drag queen' (van Klinken 2019: 59). Barasa released a single in 2015 with singer Noti Flow called *Same Love*, and the music video featured LGBTQ+ activists from across Africa, with the aim of making LGBTQ+ people visible and represented in mainstream spaces. The video was banned nationally in Kenya. This demonstrates the challenging impact of activist work in hostile spaces; yet despite the ban, the presence and absence of the work has turned up the volume on broader discussions about human rights and equality.

In the UK, Muslim drag queen Asifa LaHore is an activist for the 'gaysian' (gay Asian) community. A 2015 documentary (Channel 4) about LaHore's work sparked controversy with a fear of backlash against LaHore, which included threats against her life. LaHore was speaking out about a lack of support and organisations for LGBTQ+ Muslims, who had formed a hidden population. LaHore is able to reconcile her drag performance, her trans identity, and her sexuality, through an individualised interpretation of the beliefs and practices. In her analysis of LaHore's impact on drag, Claire Pamment writes, 'Asifa's performances open doors for considering the possibilities that Islam offers for queerness and transness' (2021: 116). LaHore says:

> For me it has never been an issue in terms of how I practice what I interpret as Islam ... I fast, I pray, I believe in one god, I give to charity, I've been on pilgrimage. All I do know is I exist. I'm gay, I'm Muslim, I'm a drag queen, I'm British, I'm a Pakistani. People say that all these things shouldn't fit right together but hey, here I am.
>
> (Asifa LaHore, cited in Sweney 2015)

Similarly, Val Qaeda is another UK based Muslim drag queen who makes clear how Asian and Muslim queens are underrepresented in drag spaces. Qaeda describes how they receive messages of support from countries where it remains illegal to be gay, yet where people are able to connect digitally with her work. Qaeda's description of her drag work seeks to offer religious literacy to those who know little about Islam, and busts some stereotypes about Muslim people:

> South Asians and Muslims aren't these scary … people who want a world of arranged marriages and no bacon. We're not a monolith. … We often keep ourselves to ourselves and stay within our community because that's where a lot of us feel safe. Surrounding ourselves with people who share our culture simply because it's easier. My drag allows you to take a peek behind the Burkha. You get to see the conversations we have behind closed doors. We get horny, we have sex, we like to have fun.
>
> (Val Qaeda, cited in Rabinowitz 2022)

It is interesting to note how Abrahamic traditions (Judaism, Christianity, Islam) are based on patriarchy and have an uncomfortable history with LGBTQ+ individuals. Even in denominations or movements that have taken steps to accept and affirm LGBTQ+ people, the history of religion and non-normative gender and sexuality is a difficult one. Conversely, Dharmic traditions show variations.

In Hinduism, there are examples of gods who are gender fluid; the Kama Sutra discusses same-sex relationships, yet colonial influences have introduced more hostile teachings that persist. Durga Gawde, for example, is an Indian artist and activist, incorporating their gender-fluid identity into their performance work (Mehra 2020). While it would be incorrect to align this with 'drag' in the Western sense, Gawde's performance work is a visible call for inclusion for LGBTQ+ people, and they often draw inspiration from Hindu mythology in their work. Equally, Maya The Drag Queen from India incorporates Hindu mythology and faith-based aesthetics into their drag (Siganporia 2019). Maya often draws on depictions from goddesses like Durga and Kali. Within South Asian communities, hijras are recognised as a distinct third-gender community with spiritual significance. While hijras are not 'drag', they demonstrate that gender and sexual fluidity has a long cultural, social and spiritual history.

While religion is often protected under local laws, it is a significant force that continues to challenge the rights of LGBTQ+ people to exist in some contexts, and often wades in on debates around non-normative genders and sexualities. It is therefore important to recognise how activist activities can counter these narratives, including the persistence of faith among LGBTQ+ people. In *RuPaul's Drag Race*, there is the example of Mo Heart, season ten, who discusses how their faith impacts on their drag. Equally, RuPaul asks for an 'Amen!' at the end of each episode of *RuPaul's Drag Race*.

DRAG ACTIVISM FOR SEXUAL HEALTH (HIV/AIDS)

HIV (human immunodeficiency virus) is a condition that affects a person's immune system and their ability to fight off infection. AIDS (acquired immune deficiency syndrome) is the most advanced stage of HIV infection, when the immune system is severely damaged and life-threatening infections or cancers can occur. While AIDS cannot be transmitted from one person to the other, HIV can, and it is often transmitted via bodily fluids during sexual activity. Today, with early diagnosis and effective treatments, most people with HIV will not develop any AIDS-related illnesses and can live their lives managing the condition, but this was not always the case during the early years of the HIV/AIDS epidemic.

During the 1980s and 1990s, while coming out as gay, lesbian, bisexual or trans was still an issue given the heteronormative and cis-normative social climates, revealing one's status as living with HIV or AIDS was a double stigma. The very fact that the condition is associated with sexual activity makes it difficult to discuss. Very little research exists on drag performers who did disclose such personal health details, often with the objective of raising consciousness and awareness, given the denial of real health care and research into the disease. In one example from Taylor and Rupp's ethnographic study, they say that one of their participants, Scabola Feces, 'is HIV-positive, is thin, and has large expressive eyes, a raspy smoker's voice, and a big evil-sounding laugh' (Taylor & Rupp 2005: 245). They later note how, as researchers, they honoured the decision to edit out some discussions that the drag queens wanted to omit, including Scabola's details on how HIV affects his life. They state specifically that 'Scabola regrets that the book leaves that out' (2005: 252). Clearly there is potential for vulnerability in revealing one's health conditions so publicly.

Yet, as HIV has been a condition that has affected members of the LGBTQ+ community, activism around the condition, including by drag performers, has been essential to raise education, awareness and treatment. Today, the outlook for those with HIV is much better than 30–40 years ago. Drag activism can be seen in Jeffrey Bennett and Isaac West's (2009) study on the Armorettes (www.thearmorettes.com), an Atlanta-based drag group that were activist in the fight against HIV/AIDS in the south. The group combined entertainment with HIV/AIDS activism, using their performance shows to raise money and donating every cent of their tips to combat the epidemic and its associated stigma. One performer, Jim Marks (aka Bubba D. Licious) describes his own personal motivations for this: 'We were in the height of it. I can remember going to Patterson's Funeral Home for five consecutive days in 1990 … I became an Armorette because of my desire to help. I couldn't write a check for all I wanted to give' (Bennett & West 2009: 306). The drag queens service to the LGBTQ+ community of Atlanta continues to this day.

In 1992, Chicago-based drag queen Joan Jett Blakk ran for political office to draw attention to HIV/AIDS awareness. Joe Jeffreys describes this as 'throwing his wig into the race for president' (1993: 186), and Blakk took part in media interviews, as all nominees for elections do, raising issues of gender, race and sexuality at each opportunity (Illinois History & Lincoln Collections 2018). Similarly, many members of the activist group ACT UP, used their drag performances to challenge societal norms and draw attention to the urgent need for HIV/AIDS education and healthcare.

RuPaul's Drag Race has afforded the opportunity for drag queens to speak out to de-stigmatise HIV. From Ongina in the first series in 2009, to Trinity K. Bonet in the sixth series in 2014, these disclosures provided visibility to the condition and served to educate viewers. Across the Atlantic, in season three of *RuPaul's Drag Race UK*, Charity Kase became a visible figure in HIV/AIDS advocacy after her own diagnosis, using her platform to speak openly about living with HIV and helping to reduce stigma (Day 2021).

De Sousa et al. (2024) explore the perception of Brazilian drag queens in relation to the social representation of HIV/AIDS. Despite advances in medical treatments and education programmes, a number of queens in the study express concerns about the persistent stigma surrounding HIV/AIDS, particularly within the LGBTQ+ community.

The participants state a need for education and prevention, especially within the queer community, and they highlight the need for advocacy-based work to remove shame and stigma. They argue that the stigma is worse than the condition itself, and it stops people from getting tested or treated. The authors advocate for better healthcare access and more inclusive health policies. Through public policy, conversations and support networks can be created to fight the stigma.

MENTAL HEALTH ADVOCACY

Given the hostile and distressingly high risks of abuse and violence related to hate crimes against LGBTQ+ people, it is sadly unsurprising that mental health issues are prevalent in the community. According to the Trevor Project (2022), 45% of LGBTQ+ youth seriously considered attempting to take their own lives and rates of mental health struggles are higher among transgender and non-binary youth compared to their cisgender peers (Trevor Project 2022). Discrimination, stigma, family, and peer rejection are widely experienced among LGBTQ+ people, with limited sources of support.

Such discussions around mental ill-health, anxiety and depression sit in sharp contrast to the fabulously flamboyant world of drag, yet these two extremes have important intersections. The impact of drag performers opening up about their own experiences and struggles of mental ill-health helps to raise awareness and generate compassionate conversations in a call to support. *RuPaul's Drag Race* has also helped spotlight some of these struggles (Nichols 2018). On the programme, the 'werkroom' conversations between contestants often shed light on the personal and emotional aspects behind the drag. Polynesian queen, Brita, from season twelve (USA) was open about her mental health challenges. She details how, in 2023, she was admitted to a psychiatric ward for a month due to severe struggles and later suffered a heart attack. In line with the principles of self-love advocated in *Drag Race*, Brita makes an important call for individuals to prioritise mental health.

Drag performer Alex Jenny blogs about how drag helped their journey to wellness. They write:

> Finding a community that uplifted me and saw me for who I truly was helped my mental health immensely. It's hella stressful

when you're hiding parts of yourself that don't conform to societal expectations of how you should identify … You don't feel like a full human. But being able to come out and step into your authentic self relieves that pressure and stress so that you can explore what feels authentic to you.

(Jenny 2023)

Within the UK, a number of drag kings are known for their commitment to raising public consciousness and awareness around mental health, and advocating for inclusive and supportive queer spaces. Yas Necati is a writer, activist, and drag king (who is also known as Turkish pop star, Tarkan) and advocates for stronger mental health provision for LGBTQ+ people. They state the importance of self-care in dealing with mental ill-health (Necati 2022). Equally, drag king, Beau Jangles, used to be a mental health social worker (Gavin 2022).

Cherry Valentine: Gypsy Queen and Proud is a 2022 BBC Three documentary that focuses on Cherry Valentine (performed by George Ward), who was eliminated in episode two of season two of *RuPaul's Drag Race UK*. The documentary focuses on how Ward navigates the complexities of reconciling Romani Traveller heritage and identity as a queer drag performer. Ward had previously worked as a qualified mental health nurse, and openly discusses the internal conflicts and isolation that formed part of his teenage years. He is reflective about the struggles of being LGBTQ+ within the Traveller community, noting that these feelings led to periods of depression and suicidal thoughts. Tragically, George Ward died by suicide on 18 September 2022 at the age of 28 (Wratten 2023). The documentary stands as an emotive tribute to Ward's bravery in tackling issues of identity reconciliation, and his advocacy for mental health awareness within LGBTQ+ and drag communities.

CLIMATE CHANGE

Animal rights campaigners and those concerned with environmental disasters and global warming engage in activism, and a number of drag performers can be counted among the advocates. Pattie Gonia, the drag persona created and performed by Wyn Wiley, describes themselves as an environmental activist. Combining their artistry and advocacy as 'intersectional environmentalism', Wiley can be seen calling for ethical decisions around excessive waste and consumerism, as they write about Pattie:

> She is the utmost representation of me and how I care for the planet – whether it's wearing a wig made of 100 pieces of trash, or normalising outfit repeating, or only having 4 wigs as opposed to 40. Drag is a space with so much stuff in it, so I say to myself, 'how can I fight against that consumerism?' (Campbell 2020).

Pattie's performance draws attention to how all performance art can often create waste. Drag performers particularly often use a lot of materials in their costumes and shows, which can contribute to environmental consequences. In 2024, Pattie hosted the 'Save Her!' drag show for New York Climate Week. In this performance, Pattie projected the faces of global billionaire tycoons profiteering from oil production. Pattie names these as 'Oil Criminals' and under the images projected was the caption 'These are the men who are killing us' (Allaire 2024). While tackling serious issues head on and speaking truth to power, Pattie is also able to infuse recycled fashion, joy, laughter, camp and artistry into climate activism. So impactful was this public protest that the influential fashion magazine *Vogue* covered the events.

Honey LaBronx has used her spotlight to advocate for veganism and is also known as 'The Vegan Drag Queen', based in New York, USA. LaBronx has a successful social media presence, including a YouTube channel sharing vegan recipes and cooking. LaBronx describes her mission as follows: 'I love bringing my animal rights message to places where people aren't necessarily expecting it. The novelty of watching a drag queen lead a cooking demo can spark a great conversation that otherwise might never happen' (Prater 2019).

Equally, contestants who have appeared on *RuPaul's Drag Race* have been able to mobilise their new-found fame to spotlight animal rights and call for cruelty-free products. These include Scaredy Kat (UK), who attends London animal rights marches, and states about fur 'None of us know why we're here on this planet, so why is one life more important than the other? … You wouldn't kill your cat and put it on a coat, so why should you kill a fox or, like, a mink or anything else? Because there's not really any difference'

(PETA UK 2020). There are others who combine artistry with activism when it comes to animal rights: Bimini Bon Boulash (UK), Alaska Thunderfuck, Kim Chi, Heidi N Closet, among others (Prater 2019).

CONCLUSION

Drag studies remains interdisciplinary – there is no natural home for drag or queer studies, given that its disruptive agenda is potent and far-reaching. Scholars researching drag come from a number of different disciplinary backgrounds, and with this, bring interesting and multi-disciplinary lenses to the critical study of drag performances and practices. Academics also come from a varying degree of social and cultural backgrounds, with different concerns and critiques relating to their own identities, or to communities and groups for which they are allies and advocates.

Drag studies in the academy has shone fresh light on existing practices, all of which are products of problematic social and cultural histories. One further commitment for scholars working in drag studies must continue to include ethnographic practices. Viviane Namaste rightly called out Butler's theories of gender subversion, which were formulated without actually speaking to real people who subvert gender. Namaste states how Butler's theory 'would be well served by actually speaking with everyday women about their lives' (Namaste 2009: 25). There are some excellent examples of research studies co-created with drag performers. Leila J. Rupp and Verta Taylor's pivotal text *Drag Queens at the 801 Cabaret* (2003) paid careful attention to the living experiences of drag performers, including an exploration of some of the critical concerns that shaped their lives and performance practices. More recently, Katie Horowitz's study on drag kings and drag queens in Ohio (Horowitz 2020) explores the divergences and differences between the two communities to offer an assessment of how each category of the queer umbrella operates with varying agendas and politics. While the recent surge in drag scholarship has rightly explored mainstream representations, due to the cultural explosion of drag in the media (including the vast quantity of critical analysis based on *RuPaul's Drag Race*), ethnographic practices allow scholars to continue to investigate the multiple layers of drag practices that are not always visible onscreen due to the limitations, bias or exclusionary practices discussed in this chapter. While RuPaul Charles may have the monopoly on drag franchises in the mainstream media, the intersectional analysis in this chapter makes clear that he certainly does not have the monopoly on drag!

Drag is a political art form that is able to bend and flex in creative ways to address some of the most urgent problems in society. The personal experiences of the drag performer, including their characteristics, motivate their engagement with activism. It is important to note that speaking out often comes with a price. Many industry and commercial forms do not want to associate themselves with outspoken advocates, and prefer to use brand-ambassadors who are more neutral in their political allegiances. Consequently, capitalism often gets in the way of change.

While it would be wrong to claim all drag is activist, there is a certain disruption to all drag performance that is counter-cultural, subversive, and challenges the status quo in terms of gender perceptions. This chapter has offered some concise case studies of the important activist work from a number of artists and performers committed to fighting injustices. In this way, drag is more than performance or entertainment, it is part of wider activist movements, protests, consciousness-raising and advocacy. Pairing drag with activism often places a lot of pressure on drag performers in ways that we do not with other artists; there is an expectation, and with that comes burden, as Stokoe points out (2020a). For many though, activism comes with the job. As one participant in Berbary and Johnson's study on drag kings exclaims, 'So do it. Do drag with love, passion, and respect. Do it all? Yes we can' (2016: 310).

FURTHER READING/RESOURCES

DRAG THEORY

Barker, M. J. & Scheele, J. (2016) Queer: A Graphic History. London: Icon Books. Readers can trace the academic and activist journey of queer theory in this graphic book. (remove -s from books, too) Sections include intersectionality, identity politics, trans rights.

Crenshaw, K. (2016). 'The Urgency of Intersectionality'. TED Talk. Retrieved from https://www.youtube.com/watch?v=akOe5-UsQ2o. In this TED Talk, Crenshaw discusses how overlapping identities such as race, gender, and class compound an individual's experiences of discrimination. This video explains the importance of intersectionality in the pursuit of social justice.

Stokoe, K. (2020). *Reframing Drag: Beyond Subversion and the Status Quo.* **Abingdon: Routledge.** Drawing on detailed research and theory, Stokoe explores how drag can both resist and reinforce dominant gender norms. This is a must-read text for readers wanting to pay close attention to how drag is framed, as Stokoe urges a more complex, critical reading of drag culture.

DRAG ISSUES AND ACTIVISM

Fitzgerald, T. & Marquez, L. (2020). *Legendary Children.* **New York: Penguin.** This text takes a deep dive into drag history and its ties to LGBTQ+ activism, framed through the lens of *RuPaul's Drag Race.*

Khubchandani, K. (2023) *Decolonize Drag.* **New York: OR Books.** This critical exploration of drag beyond Western norms is a must-read. Khubchandani highlights the colonial histories and global resistance inherent in drag.

Lawson, J. & Lloyd Knight, E. 2019. *Rainbow Revolutions. Power, Pride and Protest in the Fight for Queer Rights.* **London: Hachette.** This is a visually engaging, accessible history of LGBTQ+ activism, celebrating key moments of pride and protest.

GLOSSARY

Ableism Discrimination against disabled people and favouring of non-disabled people.

Black Lives Matter An anti-racist movement pushing for racial justice and an end to police violence.

Camp An aesthetic that thrives on exaggeration.

Cisnormativity The assumption that everyone is cisgender (identifies with their sex assigned at birth).

Essentialism The belief that identity traits (like gender) are fixed and natural, rather than shaped by culture and context.

Fat Studies An academic field that challenges anti-fat bias and explores how bodies are treated in culture and media.

Gender performativity The idea that gender is not something we are, but something we do, repeatedly.

Heteronormativity The assumption that everyone is heterosexual.

Homonormativity Where queer culture attempts to mirror straight norms.

Intersectionality   A way of seeing how systems of power (like racism, sexism, classism) combine to result in multiple marginalisations.

Killjoy feminism   Sara Ahmed's term for feminists who make things awkward by calling out injustice.

#MeToo movement   A feminist global push against sexual harassment and assault, led by survivors and grounded in the demand for change.

Misogyny   Hatred, mistrust, or devaluing of women.

Patriarchy   A system where men hold most of the power and shape rules.

Socialisation   The lifelong process where individuals learn the norms, values, and behaviours expected in their society.

Stonewall Riots   The 1969 protests in New York sparked by queer and trans resistance to police raids, widely seen as a turning point in LGBTQ+ rights.

Transphobia   Fear, hatred, or mistreatment of trans people.

REFERENCES

Ahmed, S. (2017). *Living a Feminist Life*. Durham, NC: Duke University Press.

Allaire, C. (2024). 'Pattie Gonia's Environmental Drag Show Was "Anti-Plastic Fantastic"'. British Vogue. Retrieved from www.vogue.co.uk/gallery/pattie-gonia-climate-week-drag-show (accessed June 2025).

Barrett, R. (1998). 'Indexing Polyphonous Identity in the Speech of African American Drag Queens'. In Bucholtz, M., Liang, A. C., & Sutton, L., A. (eds), *Reinventing Identities: The Gendered Self In Discourse*, 313–326. New York: Oxford University Press.

Benner, J. & Grove, J. (2023). 'New NISVS Data on Sexual Violence and Sexual Identity: Key Findings and Prevention Recommendations'. National Sexual Violence Resource Center (NSVRC). Retrieved from https://www.nsvrc.org/blogs/new-nisvs-data-sexual-violence-and-sexual-identity-key-findings-and-prevention (accessed June 2025).

Bennett, J., & West, I. (2009). '"United we stand, divided we fall": AIDS, Armorettes, and the Tactical Repertoires of Drag', *Southern Communication Journal*, 74(3), 300–313.

Berbary, L. A. & Johnson, C. W. (2016). 'En/Activist Drag: Kings Reflect on Queerness, Queens, and Questionable Masculinities', *Leisure Sciences*, 39(4), 305–318.

Butler, J. (1988). 'Performative Acts and Gender Constitution: An Essay in Phenomenology and Feminist Theory'. *Theatre Journal*, 40(4), 519–531.

Butler, J. (1990). *Gender Trouble*. London: Routledge.

Butler, J. (1993). *Bodies That Matter: On The Discursive Limits Of Sex*. London: Routledge.

Butler, J. (1999). 'Gender is Burning: Questions of Appropriation and Subversion'. In Thornham, S. (ed.), *Feminist Film Theory*, 336–349. Edinburgh: Edinburgh University Press.

Campbell, M. (2020). 'Meet Pattie Gonia: An Environmental Drag Queen on a Mission'. Euronews. Retrieved from https://www.euronews.com/green/2020/10/22/meet-pattie-gonia-an-environmental-drag-queen-on-a-mission (accessed June 2025).

Congregation for the Doctrine of the Faith. (1984). 'Letter to the Bishops of the Catholic Church on the Pastoral Care of Homosexual Persons'. Retrieved from https://www.vatican.va/roman_curia/congregations/cfaith/documents/rc_con_cfaith_doc_19861001_homosexual-persons_en.html (accessed June 2025).

Cooper, C. (2016). *Fat Activism: A Radical Social Movement*. Bristol: Hammer On Press.

Crenshaw, K. (1991). 'Mapping the Margins: Intersectionality, Identity Politics, and Violence against Women of Color', *Stanford Law Review*, 43(6), 1241–1299.

Day, H. (2021). 'Drag Race UK's Charity Kase: 'Using My Platform to Speak Out about HIV Stigma'. BBC Three. Retrieved from https://www.bbc.co.uk/bbcthree/article/a536d462-6272-4688-827d-d17d63d20fdf. (accessed June 2025).

de Beauvoir, S. (2009). *The Second Sex*. Trans. Constance Borde and Sheila Malovany-Chevallier. New York: Alfred A. Knopf.

de Lauretis, T. (1991). 'Queer Theory: Lesbian and Gay Sexualities An Introduction', *Differences*, 3(2): iii–xviii.

de Sousa, T. T., de Araújo, L. F., de Sousa Lima Filho, G., da Silva Alves, M. E., & da Silva Sousa, E. M. (2024). 'O Que Pensam As Drag Queens Brasileiras Acerca Da HIV/Aids? Suas Representações Sociais', *Revista Brasileira de Estudos da Homocultura*, 7(22).

Drysdale, K. (2019). *Intimate Investments in Drag King Cultures: The Rise and Fall of a Lesbian Social Scene*. Cham, Switzerland: Palgrave Macmillan.

Edward, M. (2012). Council House Movie Star. Retrieved from www.youtube.com/watch?reload=9&v=TR_AR2Qg3Rk (accessed June 2025).

Edward, M. (2018). *Mesearch and the Performing Body*. London: Palgrave Macmillan.

Edward, M. & Farrier, S. (eds). (2020). *Contemporary Drag Practices and Performers: Drag in a Changing Scene Volume 1*. London: Bloomsbury Publishing.

Edward, M. & Farrier, S. (eds). (2021). *Drag Histories, Herstories and Hairstories: Drag in a Changing Scene Volume 2*. London: Bloomsbury Publishing.

Edward, M. & Farrier, S. (eds). (2025). *Drag Vistas and Visions: Drag in a Changing Scene, Volume 3*. London: Bloomsbury Publishing.

Ehlers Danlos Society (2019). 'Yvie Oddly wins RuPaul's Drag Race 11 and the Hearts of the EDS Community'. Retrieved from https://www.ehlers-danlos.com/yvie-oddly-wins-drag-race-11/ (accessed June 2025).

Fileborn, B., & Loney-Howes, R. (eds). (2019). *# MeToo and the Politics of Social Change*. Cham, Switzerland: Springer Nature.

Fitzgerald, T. and Marquez, L. (2020). *Legendary Children*. New York: Penguin.

Flood, A. (2019). 'Protest Seeks to Stop US Libraries Supporting Drag Queen Story Hour'. The Guardian. Retrieved from https://www.theguardian.com/books/2019/aug/07/protest-seeks-to-stop-us-libraries-supporting-drag-queen-story-hour (accessed June 2025).

Foucault, M. (1977). *Discipline and Punish: The Birth of the Prison*, New York: Random House.

Frye, M. (1983). 'Lesbian Feminism and the Gay Rights Movement: Another View of Male Supremacy, Another Separatism'. In Frye, M. (ed.), *The Politics of Reality*, 128–151. Berkeley: Crossing Press.

Gavin, R. (2022). 'Long Live the Drag Kings'. Hunger. Retrieved from https://hungermag.com/editorial/long-live-the-drag-kings (accessed June 2025).

González, J. C. & Cavazos K. C., (2016). 'Serving Fishy Realness: Representations of Gender Equity on RuPaul's Drag Race', *Continuum*, 30(6), 659–669.

Greenough, C. (2019). *Queer Theologies: The Basics*. Abingdon: Routledge.

Greenough, C. (2020). 'Queer Activism in the Biblical Studies Classroom', *Journal of Interdisciplinary Biblical Studies*, 2(1), 107–126.

Halberstam, J. (1998). *Female Masculinity*. North Carolina: Duke University Press.

Halperin, D. M. (1995). *Saint Foucault: Towards a Gay Hagiography*. New York: Oxford University Press.

Harper, P., Francis, B. E., Cerullo, M. (1993). 'Multi/Queer/Culture', *Radical America*, 24(4), 27–37.

hooks, b. (2009). 'Is Paris Burning?' In b. hooks, *Reel to Real: Race, Sex and Class at the Movies*, 214–226. New York: Routledge.

Horowitz, K. (2020). *Drag, Interperformance, and the Trouble with Queerness*. Abingdon: Routledge.

Human Rights Campaign. (n.d.). 'Understanding Poverty in the LGBTQ+ Community'. Retrieved from www.hrc.org/resources/understanding-poverty-in-the-lgbtq-community (accessed June 2025).

Illinois History & Lincoln Collections (2018). 'Joan Jett Blakk: Drag Queen for President'. Retrieved from https://publish.illinois.edu/ihlc-blog/2018/06/15/joan-jett-blakk-drag-queen-for-president/ (accessed June 2025).

Jagger, G. (2008). *Judith Butler: Sexual Politics, Social Change and the Power of the Performative*. London: Routledge.

Jagose, A. (1996). *Queer Theory: An Introduction*. New York: NYU Press.

Jeffreys, J. E. (1993). 'Joan Jett Blakk for President: Cross-Dressing at the Democratic National Convention', *The Drama Review*, 37(3), 186–195.

Jenny, A. (2023). 'How Drag Shows Helped Alex Jenny's Mental Health'. Wondermind. Retrieved from www.wondermind.com/article/alex-jenny (accessed June 2025).

Khubchandani, K. (2023). *Decolonize Drag*. New York: OR Books.

Lander-Cavallo, A. & Lander-Cavallo, A. (2025). 'Camp Quips: Drag, Access and Queer Crip Joy as an Act of Resistance'. In Edward, M. & Farrier, S. (eds), *Drag Vistas and Visions Drag in a Changing Scene Volume 3*, 123–144. London: Bloomsbury.

Lawson, J. and Lloyd Knight, E. 2019. *Rainbow Revolutions. Power, Pride and Protest in the Fight for Queer Rights*. London: Hachette.

Litwiller, F. (2020). 'Normative Drag Culture and the Making of Precarity', *Leisure Studies*, 39(4), 600–612.

Lööv, A. O. (2015). 'The (Ab)uses of Gender Trouble in Feminist Drag King Activism in Sweden in the Early 2000s', *lambda nordica*, 20(2–3), 96–124.

Mehra, S. (2020). 'In Conversation With Durga Gawde: An Artist, Activist And Drag King'. Feminism in India. Retrieved from https://feminis-minindia.com/2020/10/19/durga-gawde-an-artist-activist-and-drag-king (accessed June 2025).

Momma's Boyz Drag Kings. (2020). 'Drag King Alex U. Inn – Glory (Black Lives Matter)'. Retrieved from www.youtube.com/watch?v=hn1Mg92garI. (accessed June 2025).

Namaste, V. (2009). 'Undoing Theory: The "Transgender Question" and the Epistemic Violence of Anglo-American Feminist Theory', *Hypatia*, 24(3), 11–32.

National Museum of Ireland. (2014). 'Panti Bliss' Noble Call Speech Dress'. Retrieved from https://www.museum.ie/en-ie/collections-research/collection/resilience/artefact/panti-bliss%E2%80%99-noble-call-speech-dress/80ce1200-dd17-41b2-a0aa-e21b12e898e8 (accessed June 2025).

Necati, Y. (2022). 'Self-Care and LGBTQ+ Mental Health'. Happy Valley Pride. Retrieved from https://happyvalleypride.co.uk/whats-on/27/self-care-and-lgbtq-mental-health-with-yas-necati (accessed June 2025).

Newton, E. (1972). *Mother Camp: Female Impersonators in America*. Englewood Cliffs, NJ: Prentice-Hall.

Nichols, J. M. (2018). '*RuPaul's Drag Race* Stars Open Up About Mental Health And The Toll Of Superstardom'. HuffPost UK. Retrieved from www.huff-ingtonpost.co.uk/entry/rupauls-drag-race-mental-health_n_5a60d92ee4b0 1b82649d8594 (accessed June 2025).

Pamment, C. (2021). 'Im/possible Un/veilings: Asifa Lahore and British-Asian Muslim Drag Performance'. In Rosenberg, T. D'Urso, S., & Winget, A. R. (eds), *The Palgrave Handbook of Queer and Trans Feminisms in Contemporary Performance*, 113–131. London: Palgrave Macmillan.

PETA UK (2020). '*Drag Race* Star Scaredy Kat Keeps Paws Off Cruel Fashion'. Retrieved from www.youtube.com/watch?v=rh9s_o9f0oM&t=4s (accessed June 2025).

Pomerantz, A. (2017). 'Big-Girls Don't Cry: Portrayals Of The Fat Body In RuPaul's Drag Race'. In Brennan, N. & Gudelunas, D. (eds), *RuPaul's Drag Race and the Shifting Visibility of Drag Culture*, 103–120. London: Palgrave Macmillan.

Prater, D. (2019). 'Drag Queens Who Care About Animal Rights' PETA Blog. Retrieved from www.peta.org/news/drag-queens-vegan-animal-rights (accessed June 2025).

Rabinowitz, L. (2022). 'Val Qaeda: The Bollywood Bombshell'. *Notion*, 6 June. Retrieved from https://notion.online/val-qaeda-the-bollywood-bombshell.

Raymond, J. (1994). *The Transsexual Empire: The Making of the She-Male*. New York: Teachers College Press.

Reynolds, D. (2020). 'RuPaul's 2016 Thoughts on Black Lives Matter and Police Brutality'. Advocate. Retrieved from https://www.advocate.com/race/2020/6/09/rupauls-2016-thoughts-black-lives-matter-and-police-brutality (accessed June 2025).

Rhyne, R. (2004). 'Racializing White Drag', *Journal of Homosexuality*, 46(3–4), 181–194.

Rich, A. (1980). 'Compulsory Heterosexuality and Lesbian Existence', *Signs: Journal of Women in Culture and Society*, 5(4), 631–660.

RuPaul's Drag Race (2021). 'The Queens Of Season 12 Discuss #BlackLives Matter'. Retrieved from www.youtube.com/watch?v=XKrdezEWKig&t=33s. (accessed June 2025).

Rupp, L. J., & Taylor, V. (2003). *Drag Queens at the 801 Cabaret*. Chicago, IL: University of Chicago Press.

Rupp, L. J., Taylor, V., & Shapiro, E. L. (2010). 'Drag Queens and Drag Kings: The Difference Gender Makes', *Sexualities*, 13(3), 275–294.

Siganporia, S. (2019). 'How Maya The Drag Queen Is Using Drag to Educate and Empower Indian Audiences'. Vogue India. Retrieved from https://www.vogue.in/culture-and-living/content/maya-indian-drag-queen-alex-mathew-inspire-educate (accessed June 2025).

Sontag, S. (1983). *Notes on Camp*. London: Penguin.

Stokoe, K. (2020a). *Reframing Drag: Beyond Subversion and the Status Quo*. Abingdon: Routledge.

Stokoe, K. (2020b). 'A Transfeminist Critique of Drag Discourses and Performance Styles in Three National Contexts (US, France and UK)'. In Edward, M. & Farrier, S. (eds), *Contemporary Drag Practices and Performers: Drag in a Changing Scene Volume 1*, 87–102. London: Bloomsbury.

Strings S. & Bui L. T., (2014). 'She Is Not Acting, She Is', *Feminist Media Studies*, 14(5), 822–836.

Sweney, M. (2015). 'Muslim Drag Queens Activist Voices Fears of Backlash Over Channel 4 Film'. *The Guardian*, 18 August. Retrieved from https://www.theguardian.com/media/2015/aug/18/muslim-drag-queens-channel-4-sir-ian-mckellen-asif-quaraishi-backlash

Taylor, V. & Rupp, L. J. (2005). 'Crossing Boundaries in Participatory Action Research: Performing Protest with Drag Queens'. In Croteau, D., Hoynes, W., & Ryan, C. (eds), *Rhyming Hope and History: Activists, Academics, And Social Movement Scholarship*, 239–264. Minneapolis, MN: University of Minneapolis Press.

Trevor Project. (2022). 'National Survey on LGBTQ Youth Mental Health'. Retrieved from www.thetrevorproject.org/survey-2022 (accessed June 2025).

UCLA School of Law Williams Institute. (2022). 'LGBT People Nine Times More Likely than Non-LGBT People to be Victims of Violent Hate Crimes'. Retrieved from https://williamsinstitute.law.ucla.edu/press/lgbt-hate-crimes-press-release (accessed June 2025).

Van Klinken, Adriaan. (2019). *Kenyan, Christian, Queer. Religion, LGBT Activism and Arts of Resistance in Africa*. Pennsylvania, PA: Pennsylvania University Press.

Volcano, D. L. & Halberstam, J. (1999). *The Drag King Book*. London: Serpent's Tail.

Warner, M. (ed.). (1993). *Fear of a Queer Planet: Queer Politics and Social Theory, Volume 6*. Minnesota, MN: University of Minnesota Press.

Wilcox, M. (2018). *Queer Nuns: Religion, Activism and Serious Parody*. New York: New York University Press.

Wratten, M. (2023). 'The Life and Legacy of Cherry Valentine Star George Ward'. Pink News. Retrieved from https://www.thepinknews.com/2023/09/18/cherry-valentine-george-ward-life-legacy-drag/ (accessed June 2025).

Zylbercweig, Z. (1934). 'Litman, Pepi'. In *Leksikon fun Yidishn Teater* [Lexicon of the Yiddish Theatre; in Yiddish], vol. 2, columns 1054–1057. With the assistance of Jacob Mestel. Warsaw: Elisheva.

DRAG AND THE MEDIA

INTRODUCTION

From its roots in subcultural spaces, underground, hidden, and accessible to few, drag in the digital age has gone mainstream. Drag's relationship with various media forms is entangled with questions of representation, reception, politics, and power. Media, after all, both reflect and shape drag culture. This chapter considers how drag travels through various media formats: television, radio, film, music, and digital platforms. All of these are linked entirely to capitalism, and attention is afforded to the media 'merching' of drag.

The term 'media' is broad, so it is important to distinguish between the use, function, and impact of each communication form: from broadcast television and radio to cinema, photography, print, digital platforms, and social media networks. Each of these formats offers different and distinct modes of representation and transmission. For example, television edits for drama; TikTok cuts in seconds; Instagram is concerned with visual aesthetics. Drag, as a living art form, engages with these multiple formats to ensure widespread reach. Therefore, drag on media platforms can be considered as both a translation of the art form and a transformation of it.

One of the earliest cultural insights into the impact of the media can be seen in Marshall McLuhan's phrase, 'the medium is the message', the slogan formed the title of the first chapter of his book *Understanding Media: The Extensions of Man* (the book's title is also ironic for our purposes), published in 1964. Despite the normative, gendered, and thankfully dated use of language in the title, McLuhan's argument lives on. He argued that it is not simply content that

DOI: 10.4324/9781003431800-4

influences reception, but that the medium itself determines how a message is perceived. For McLuhan (1964), characteristics of media technology shape content and consciousness. Drag is no exception, and the art and performance forms continue to bend and flex in new, creative, transformative ways. In brief, a drag performance on a live cabaret stage is not the same performance that is purposefully shot, edited and uploaded to Instagram. The formats differ in their production and reception.

As drag moves between various media platforms, its meanings shift; what is legible, popular, or subversive in one context may fall flat or become commodified in another. In the 1980s, cultural commentator Stuart Hall demonstrated how techniques such as encoding and decoding add another layer of complexity to the transmission of content. According to Hall, media texts are not passively consumed by audiences; rather, they are infused with and encoded by producers with certain meanings. These meanings are then decoded by audiences in ways that may align with, oppose, or negotiate producers' intentions (Hall 1980). With regards to drag, this allows for multiple interpretations and individual responses, all of which are shaped by who we are, our locations, backgrounds, identities, worldviews, experiences, attitudes, and biases. Each reading is subjective and contextually located. Rather than meaning being transmitted universally with context, readers/viewers/listeners/users actually construct their own meaning and bring subjective meaning to media.

As we have seen in Chapter 1, drag insisted on its own spotlight in public spaces long before its current mainstream popularity. In the early twentieth century, for example, 'female impersonation' was a feature of vaudeville shows, often framed as novelty. Mid-century television in the Global North, detailed below, used drag to blend satire with entertainment, reaching TV audiences with very subtle references to queer life, largely built on innuendos. It is important to note that such media appearances remained the exception, and they were largely controlled by heteronormative values that enforced gatekeeping and regulation. Here, drag performers often had to walk a delicate and precarious tightrope between appealing to audiences through comedy, yet censoring queerness.

The HIV/AIDS crisis of the 1980s and early 1990s altered the stakes of drag in public life, bringing urgency, rage and a call to activism into performances. Documentaries such as Jennie Livingston's *Paris is Burning* (1990) and Frank Simon's *The Queen* (1968) provided rare glimpses into drag and ballroom subcultures, offering narratives that were emotive, intimate, and candid. These films were rare glimpses into drag and queer lives off stage, and they raised consciousness and debate around drag identity and performance.

What began as a niche competition on cable TV in the late 2000s evolved into a global media empire, as *RuPaul's Drag Race* (*RPDR*) propelled drag into mainstream popular culture. We argue that this success is a paradox. Drag has its roots in anti-normativity and queerness, so any assimilation to the mainstream could potentially dilute the subversive potential of drag. While the show has brought drag to unprecedented levels of visibility, and can even be commended for its public education on LGBTQ+ experiences, Chapter 2 details how it has also been critiqued for a number of intersectional issues, and its role in turning a community art form into a corporate product (Brennan & Gudelunas 2017; Khubchandani 2023).

This chapter considers drag by media form: television, radio, film/online video, social media and digital drag, in order to attempt to reflect historical content related to how drag has been produced, edited, distributed, and consumed. Yet, this chapter cannot cover every TV show and film depicting drag! Indeed, drag on TV and film necessitates a whole book in itself. Jean-Louis Ginibre's book *Ladies or Gentlemen, A Pictorial History of Male Cross Dressing in the Movies* (2005) is one such example devoted to such histories, with a specific focus on drag queens. In the case studies we analyse below, it is striking how each platform brings with it specific aesthetics, preferences, and politics. Understanding drag across various media forms requires close analysis alongside a broader understanding of the cultural technologies at play.

Drag resists being confined to a single media form. While performers move between media platforms and across physical and digital spaces, drag itself has long circulated through diverse cultural histories. Although *RuPaul's Drag Race* now airs in more than 20 countries, its global presence represents just one star in a much wider constellation of drag cultures. The fluidity of drag's position in media forms is undoubtedly and problematically shaped by colonial legacies. Dominant cultural frameworks for drag creates a normativity that should be resisted when drag is viewed only in terms of its mainstream success.

What follows is a simple, but critical cartography that traces drag across television, radio, film, and digital platforms. We question how drag appears and is received across these media; as well as how drag transforms, and is transformed by the opportunities and limits of contemporary media.

DRAG ON TELEVISION

Within drag histories, the art and performance form were largely subcultural, hidden from mainstream viewings and restricted to specific performance spaces and contexts. Accordingly, television has been a crucial tool to enhance the visibility, popularity and commercialisation of drag performance. The media form has the power to catapult drag performers into global fame, yet, as we have seen in Chapter 2, this often limits drag to formats that prioritise particular bodies, aesthetics, narratives and privileged markers of identity. In this exploration of drag on television, we are largely limited to examples from English-speaking contexts that reflect our own access to these sources. The sections that follow explore televised drag across the USA, UK, Canada, Australia, and Aotearoa (New Zealand), considering both mainstream success and ongoing exclusions.

THE USA: FROM CULT FIGURE TO GLOBAL FRANCHISE

Drag on TV traces its origins to variety shows, comedy specials, and sitcoms from the mid-twentieth century onwards, where it was typically framed as humorous, absurd, or transgressive. Here, the notion of drag as gender performativity was limited, and the form was one of entertainment. One of the earliest and most enduring tropes involved cisgender male comedians donning women's clothing to provoke laughter or discomfort. For example, Milton Berle, one of American television's earliest stars, frequently appeared in drag on *Texaco Star Theater* in the late 1940s and early 1950s. His popularity was so great, he was called 'Uncle Miltie,' and used exaggerated femininity as slapstick, gesturing at the taboo of gender disruption without ever challenging its underlying norms (Horowitz 1997).

This comedic drag tradition continued through shows like *Flip Wilson* (1970–1974), where Clerow 'Flip' Wilson Jr. played Geraldine Jones, a confident, flirtatious Black woman. Unlike earlier portrayals, Geraldine had a degree of agency and self-awareness, yet despite her flirtation, she remained loyal to her unseen fictional boyfriend 'Killer'. She had a number of one liners, including 'when you're hot, you're hot; when you're not, you're not', and 'the Devil made me do it!'. Wilson is one of the best examples of drag working at the intersections of identity and performance in terms of gender and race. In one interview, he states, 'I wanted to relate to women, but didn't want to knock women … the comics were knocking women. I wanted to make my character the heroine of the story' (cited in Sutherland & Wilson 2008: 73). Wilson was notoriously private offscreen. He married twice and had five children.

Similarly, *The Carol Burnett Show* (1967–1978) frequently used drag in skits, with actors like Harvey Korman and Tim Conway donning drag for punchlines. These portrayals shaped public perceptions of drag as something theatrical, deviant, or unserious, reinforcing the idea that gender play was either laughable or safely fictional.

One important but often overlooked site of early televisual drag included portrayals of the ballroom scene in New York, which occasionally broke into the mainstream via documentary or news formats. Though not comedy, these glimpses, like Frank Simon's *The Queen* (1968), offered rare moments of authentic queer self-representation. From 1976 to 1979, *The Emerald City* show aired on New York's Channel J, appealing to LGBTQ+ audiences, with interviews from Divine and John Waters demonstrating its popularity. On the show, drag performers discussed the artistry and politics of their performances, laying the groundwork for later drag documentaries like *Paris is Burning* (1990).

Thus, before RuPaul's ascent to world media drag domination, televised drag was known for its comedy, caricature, and campness, yet it remained largely framed around parodying gendered stereotypes. These presentations were safely confined to screens and stage, but would rarely occur off stage, and if they did, would not have the same popularity or reception. Here, drag was framed largely as a gag than a legitimate art form, shaped by predominantly white, cisgender male media producers and audiences. Yet these performances, however limited, also paved the way for drag's popularity among various audiences outside of cabaret bars and pubs.

The 1990s marked a shift from comedy with the rise of RuPaul Charles, who projected glamour through hosting and music. RuPaul's hit single *Supermodel (You Better Work)* had international success and RuPaul presented subsequent MTV shows, including *The RuPaul Show* (1996–1998). Moving from the clubs to the mainstream, RuPaul introduced a high-camp, self-aware drag persona to late-night cable audiences – this was drag not for camp comedy, but for queer, and later mainstream, culture.

THE RISE AND REACH OF *RUPAUL'S DRAG RACE*

Since its debut on Logo TV in 2009, *RuPaul's Drag Race* has redefined the relationship between drag and television. Arguably, *Drag Race* signalled drag's entry into the mainstream, and certainly the global entertainment economy. As Brennan and Gudelunas argue, *RuPaul's Drag Race* represents 'the mainstreaming of queerness under neoliberal logics, turning queer subculture into consumable spectacle' (2017: 8).

Drag Race packages drag for mass appeal, while still foregrounding queerness (Brennan & Gudelunas 2017). What began as a niche reality competition show, with Vaseline-smeared camera lenses and low-budget charm, quickly grew into a global cultural machine. The show now spans multiple platforms (VH1, MTV, WOW Presents Plus), and features dozens of international spin-offs that have launched a huge number of careers. As of season seventeen, which premiered on 3 January 2025, a total of 228 contestants have competed on the original American series of *Drag Race*. Globally, the *Drag Race* franchise has expanded to include 20 localised versions, bringing the total number of contestants worldwide to over 600. At the time of writing, the *RuPaul's Drag Race* franchise has official versions in the United States, Chile, Thailand, the United Kingdom, Canada, the Netherlands, Australia and New Zealand, Spain, Italy, France, the Philippines, Belgium, Sweden, Mexico, Brazil, Germany, and South Africa.

The show's success lies in its ability to blend performance, makeover culture, and reality competition. Its hybrid format depicts drag behind the scenes with polished performances through the various runways and challenges. The ingredients of the show include talent competitions, challenges, runway looks and they are all punctuated with contestant commentary in the form of confessionals. Each episode is structured in formulaic ways, with predictable lines from RuPaul, including 'start your engines', 'it's time to lip-sync for your life', 'hash tag drag race', 'can I get an 'amen' up in here?'. The show's finale is a lip-sync duel, in which the winning contestant is told 'shantay you stay', while the loser must 'sashay away'. These lip-syncs have become one of the show's most iconic features.

While the show celebrates creativity and resilience, it has also been critiqued for its politics of inclusion (see Chapter 2). *Drag Race* has undeniably shifted drag into mainstream consciousness. It has created new economies in relation to merch, tours, podcasts, brand deals, and inspired an entire generation of performers. At the same time, many queer artists have deliberately distanced themselves from the *Drag Race* franchise, building independent drag scenes that reject its commercialised aesthetics, rigid structures, and celebrity hierarchies. These artists critique a system that rewards polish, marketability, and conformity – all of which focus on a narrow ideal of drag aesthetics, often at the expense of political engagement, local specificity, and experimental work.

CANADA: CABARET AND COMMUNITY

Early representations of drag on Canadian television have evolved from infrequent spots on public broadcast variety shows to contemporary programmes based on mentorship, education, and community building. The earliest nationally televised drag figure in Canada was Jean Guilda (1921–2012), a French-born drag queen who rose to fame on the Montréal cabaret scene during the 1950s and 1960s. In the 1970s and 1980s, Guilda was known for high-glamour acting roles in films, as well as impersonations of screen icons like Rita Hayworth and Marlene Dietrich. Guilda's celebrity status in the mainstream media marked one of the earliest examples of drag's visibility in Canada's public sphere, long before the current wave of global drag culture.

One of Guilda's contemporaries in the 1970s was Craig Russell (1948–1990). Russell originally was a hairdresser and was known for his realistic impressions of iconic stars such as Judy Garland,

Bette Davis, and Mae West. His success can be seen in his semi-autobiographical film *Outrageous!* (1977), which became one of the first internationally successful films centred on a drag queen and gay identity. The film narrates the story of a gay hairdresser-turned-drag performer and his close friend Liza, a woman living with schizophrenia. Critics praised the film for its sympathetic and caring portrayal of mental health and queer identity. Thomas Waugh (2006) places the movie in a tradition of gay Canadian media that rejects prevailing heteronormative narratives and embraces transgressive ideas. The sequel, *Too Outrageous!* (1987), did not have the same success, despite Russell's comeback. Sadly, he died of a stroke related complication from AIDS shortly after.

Drag met political comedy in the late 1980s, through the satirical TV programme *CODCO* (CBC, 1988–1993), a sketch comedy series in which performers like Greg Malone and Tommy Sexton frequently used drag to impersonate political figures (especially from the UK), including Margaret Thatcher and Queen Elizabeth II. As is the nature of political comedy, such drag performances were often critically stinging in tone. During this period, amid the HIV/AIDS crisis, drag here was able to critique power, colonialism, and authority; and, at the same time, drag was able to gatecrash into mainstream homes via the national broadcaster.

Long before the *Drag Race* franchise migrated into Canada in 2020, Canadian cable channels like PrideVision (now OutTV) created space for locally rooted drag. Documentary-style series like *Canada's a Drag* (CBC Gem, 2018–) featured queens, kings, and non-binary performers from across the country, showcasing regional cultures and centring performers who rarely appear in commercial formats (CBC Arts n.d.). Artists such as Mx. Bukuru (Edmonton), Maddie Longlegs (St. John's), and Tynomi Banks (Toronto) have been profiled through these platforms.

For contemporary audiences, *Canada's Drag Race* (Crave/OutTV, 2020–) remains perhaps the most internationally visible Canadian TV drag programme today. It follows the familiar competition format of *Drag Race*, although, notably, its casting has been more inclusive than its USA counterpart. Its first winner, Priyanka, was a mixed-race Indo-Guyanese queen. Priyanka has spoken openly about reconciling her immigrant heritage with queer visibility. The show has since featured contestants representing Black, Indigenous,

Asian, Latinx, and trans communities, including Miss Fiercalicious, Adriana, and others.

Other than *Drag Race*, what is significant about drag televised reality series in Canada is the popularity of shows that reject the competition and elimination format, in favour of creating supportive environments through mentorship. For example, the format of the series *Drag Heals* (OutTV, 2018–) is based on workshops for new drag artists. Through the space given for reflective, personal narrative, the series spotlights how drag performers explore gender identity, grief, trauma, or healing. The show culminates in live performances. Importantly, it reframes drag not only as a polished performance but showcases the private aspects of such emotional and political labour that nourish the art form.

Similarly, *Call Me Mother* (OutTV, 2021–) is based on the supportive relationship found in drag families. Mother-mentors like Peppermint, Barbada de Barbades, and Crystal guide a diverse group of emerging performers, kings/queens, non-binary, and AFAB artists, through creative challenges. Each challenge is rooted in transformation for the benefit of the queer community. Here, the show offers audiences a distinct contrast to *RuPaul's Drag Race*, reflecting the importance of drag as care rather than competition. Finally, *Slaycation* (Crave, 2024) also brings a refreshing alternative to competition-based formats. The series brings together Canadian and international queens (including BOA and Jada Shada Hudson) for a drag retreat in Ontario's Blue Mountains. Rather than a high-stakes contest, the show features the contestants at leisure, engaged in conversation, and local performance work.

Drag in Canada is also not limited to assumed adult-audiences. *The Fabulous Show with Fay and Fluffy* (Family Jr., 2022–) is a story-time cabaret variety show for preschoolers, filled with books, puppets, and animated characters. It is hosted by two Toronto-based performers. Drag here is much more than a queer performance art form for adults, as it subverts boundaries of expected audiences and critiques the arguments to do with 'exposure', linked to the push-back to drag queen story time (see Chapter 1). Drag is pedagogical, inclusive, transformative, and can engage multiple audiences across ages.

This concise overview demonstrates how drag in Canadian television has continually shifted: from glamour to gritty politics, from cabaret to children, and from competition to community. Yet what is central to the representations of drag on Canadian TV is that drag is a relational practice, serving to improve individuals and communities. The examples of Guilda's 1960s glamour, CODCO's political parody, and Fay & Fluffy's educational storytelling show how Canadian drag on screen insists on drag as something more than competition or brand, it is more about culture and community.

UNITED KINGDOM: CAMP, COMEDY, AND CLASS

Drag on British television has travelled from music hall variety shows to reality competitions. Punctuated by comedy and camp aesthetics in its early presentations, drag on UK TV has shone a spotlight on class divisions in society, and reveals distinctions between different flavours of drag, including regional variations. Historically, UK televised drag navigated a fine line between mainstream popularity and palatability, often depicted through glamour and flamboyance, as opposed to political, sexualised, or comedic forms of drag that provide social commentary.

Arthur Lucan (1885–1954) performed the role of the celebrated early drag icon, Old Mother Riley. Riley was a loud, eccentric, working-class Irish washerwoman and was popular in British variety theatre and early cinema from the 1930s to the 1950s. There were around fifteen Old Mother Riley films and numerous stage performances. The act was born out of a double act between Lucan and his wife, Kitty McShane. The focus on working-class hardships made the act popular with British audiences in post-World War II Britain. At a time when drag was largely confined to theatre, Lucan's success brought drag comedy into mainstream entertainment. His portrayal contributed to the visibility and popularity of drag as a comedic performance genre, and this undoubtedly influenced other drag forms, laying groundwork for later drag performers.

Danny La Rue was among the earliest figures to achieve drag visibility on UK television. Born in Ireland and raised in Soho, La Rue brought high-glamour costume to national stages, eventually entering living rooms via BBC specials and variety appearances. La Rue demonstrates how drag became appealing to audiences who were largely heterosexual as part of entertainment shows. Notably, La Rue was not interested in mockery or caricatures around gender in his drag (Hayward 2018). Instead, his drag was elegant, musical, and theatrical. In this way, his televised performances were successful in attracting mainstream audiences. Programmes such as *The Good Old Days* (BBC, 1953–1983), a variety programme that reimagined Edwardian music hall traditions, embodied this old-school style of British drag: high polish in terms of glamour and entertainment and low threat in terms of queerness. It did not need a finely tuned gaydar to know La Rue was gay and he was often absorbed into the respectable world of light entertainment as a popular persona. But this came at the expense of his personal life. In one programme that documents and celebrates the life and successes of celebrities, *This is Your Life* (1984), there was no reference to La Rue's partner of 37 years, who died in the same year of the broadcast. Despite the feathers and sequins that illuminated his performances, the silence on his sexuality in these forums seemed to render his drag acceptable.

John Inman was a popular camp figure on TV, not exactly a full-time drag performer in the same way as La Rue or Lily Savage (below), but his performances nonetheless shaped public perceptions of gender and queerness. Inman did leave a legacy in TV history of his camp public performances, giving glimpses at queerness on television. He was best known for his role as the flamboyant Mr Humphries in *Are You Being Served?* (BBC, 1972–1985). Inman's character was a staple of 1970s sitcom camp: mincing, innuendo-laden, and unambiguously gay. His performance has been widely debated and critiqued by some as reinforcing a narrow, desexualised stereotype of gay men as laughable and effeminate (Jeffries 2024; Needham 2007). Arguably, for a medium in which lesbian and gay performances were rare, at least this provided *some* representation, and a nod that a world beyond the *straight*-jacket of heterosexual representation exists. Beyond sitcoms, in the 1980s, Inman also performed in drag in BBC's *The Good Old Days*. These performances aligned him, even temporarily, with British drag cultures. Often drawing laughs, such performances permitted drag to enter mainstream TV programming, but often only when couched in nostalgia, camp, or comedic safety.

Televised drag in the UK was also influenced by a broader culture of cross-dressing comedy during the 1970s and 1980s, often performed by straight cisgender men in sketch shows and sitcoms. *The Dick Emery Show*, for example, had a really popular character,

Miss Mandy Dunnit, who was flirtatious and overbearing. Programmes like *Morecambe and Wise*, *The Two Ronnies*, and *Monty Python's Flying Circus* regularly featured men in wigs and dresses, but these performances seldom engaged directly with queerness. Instead, drag served as a punchline: it did not set up the joke, it was the joke. As bell hooks astutely observes, 'To choose to appear as "female" when one is "male" is always constructed in the patriarchal mindset as a loss, as a choice worthy only of ridicule' (1992: 146). Ultimately, the comedic effect of these representations was linked to a cisgender male 'lowering' his status to one of a woman, which invited laughter from audiences at the puzzlement of such a dynamic. This all served to elicit laughter within a heterosexual framework, rather than widen the horizons of gender and sexuality politics. So, while these acts did increase drag's visibility, they often reinforced stereotypes rather than challenging them.

Australian comedian Barry Humphries popularised a form of acidic comedy drag on British television in the form of Dame Edna Everage. Everage was a lilac-haired, gladioli-waving housewife-megastar from Moonee Ponds, whose comedy evolved around aloof commentary on suburban pretensions and celebrity culture. Edna's arrival on British screens in the late 1970s signalled that drag could be more than music hall spectacle or 'cross-dressing' slapstick; it could be punchy comedy. Her earliest UK appearances came via BBC specials in 1978 and 1979, but it was on ITV's *An Audience With* … series (1980, 1984, 1988) that Dame Edna fully found her format. As a solo performer, but with her silent downtrodden sidekick, Madge, Edna commanded a room of celebrity guests, mocking them mercilessly while maintaining her trademark façade of polite suburban concern. This mixture of anti-celebrity humour and camp excess was extended in *The Dame Edna Experience* (ITV, 1987–1989), a mock talk show in which Edna interviewed real guests with faux sincerity, often sending them flying through trapdoors or silencing them mid-sentence.

In the early 1990s, Edna moved further into international stardom with *Dame Edna's Hollywood* (BBC/ABC, 1991), transporting her faux-chic persona to Beverly Hills and satirising celebrity culture in the USA. Among Dame Edna's lesser-remembered television ventures was *Dame Edna's Neighbourhood Watch* (Thames Television, 1992), a reality game show in which contestants were invited into

Everage's studio, and, unknowingly, Madge and a camera crew would be at their homes, rummaging through cupboards and drawers. Everage would often mock their decor, habits, or personal items. The show was a parody of middle-class suburbia nosiness, underscored by Everage's waspish commentary. It was a parody of class, taste, and voyeurism, wrapped in glitter and delivered with Everage's trademark wink. Her final major UK appearance came in *Dame Edna Rules the Waves* (BBC One, 2019), an end-of-decade special that revisited her favourite targets with undiminished bite.

Long before *RuPaul's Drag Race* brought drag to the masses, Dame Edna had already sat down for lunch with Prime Minister Margaret Thatcher on 7 March 1982 (Margaret Thatcher Foundation n.d.), crashed the royal box at the Palladium sitting next to the then Prince Charles and Camilla in the Royal Variety Performance of 2013, and viciously parodied a number of celebrities on public TV. Culturally, Dame Edna has been framed as a paradox, both conservative and comedic. Indeed, in recent years, Humphries's legacy has been contested following widely publicised transphobic comments, which have complicated Edna's standing as a queer icon (BBC News 2019).

Everage had already marked a shift from glamour to comedy, and this was echoed with a sharper political edge in Paul O'Grady's creation, Lily Savage, who rose to popularity in the late 1980s and 1990s. Savage marked a pivotal turn towards more acerbic and abrasive comedy in televised drag. Grounded in working-class culture in Liverpool, Savage's early drag was rooted in sexually charged stand-up: raw, political, and defiantly unfiltered. Savage's appearances on *The Big Breakfast* (Channel 4, 1995–1996), and later *The Lily Savage Show* (BBC, 1997), brought class commentary to the forefront. Savage was the opposite of La Rue: instead of polite glamour, she offered tart commentary on poverty, police harassment, single motherhood, and welfare bureaucracy – all delivered in peroxide wigs and leopard print. Her presence carried a double bind: on the one hand, she shone a spotlight on the failures of the state and the lived experience of working classes; on the other, she sometimes reinforced the very stereotypes she appeared to challenge, playing into tropes of working-class people as thieves, loud-mouthed and unrespectable.

Savage's mass appeal was cemented with her hosting of *Blankety Blank* (BBC, then ITV, 1997–2002), which placed a drag queen at the very centre of prime-time family entertainment. This was a radical and pivotal move for drag representation. By this point, Savage had become a national treasure: abrasive, adored, and largely 'decent' for mainstream consumption. O'Grady eventually decided to retire Savage, yet retained public popularity with *The Paul O'Grady Show* (ITV, 2004–2009; Channel 4, 2013–2015), and later his advocacy for animal welfare on television shows and advertising campaigns.

The 1990s saw British drag and gender non-conformist representations diversify British screens, through independent films like *Beautiful Thing* (1996), late-night television segments such as *Eurotrash* (Channel 4), and documentaries exploring drag as performance art from personas such as Leigh Bowery (discussed later in this chapter). In early drag documentaries, such as *Queens for a Night* (Channel 4, 1994), audiences followed amateur drag transformations, including makeovers, costume, wigs, and preparation, all for fly-on-the-wall viewership. These shows expanded public curiosity by offering glimpses behind the curtains of performances and into the dressing rooms, an ingredient that makes *RuPaul's Drag Race* so popular today with 'werkroom' footage. More recent formats, such as *Drag SOS* (Channel 4, 2019) featuring the Family Gorgeous collective from Manchester, offer alternatives to drag competitions. Instead of lip-sync battles and eliminations, *Drag SOS* focuses on community workshops, family acceptance, and local pride. Accordingly, this format emphasises drag as a form of transformation and care, not just entertainment.

Notably absent from much of early UK televised drag were drag kings, trans performers, AFAB performers, and drag performers of colour. Even as figures like O'Grady critiqued gender roles and working-class politics, the dominant image of televised drag remained white, cisgender, and often regional. This absence continues to be challenged in newer British drag programming, including an increase in representation and diversity on *RuPaul's Drag Race UK* (BBC Three, 2019–), but it remains part of the longer legacy of representation within British media culture.

A further example is *Mrs. Brown's Boys (2011 -)*, a BBC sitcom created by and starring Brendan O'Carroll. O'Carroll plays the character of Agnes Brown through drag. The show follows the fictional lives of the loud, foul-mouthed, meddling Mrs Brown, a Dublin matriarch who gets involved in the lives of her grown-up children with chaos and comedy.

In summary, drag on British television has been polished, political, and plucky. From Danny La Rue's respectable glamour to Lily Savage's razor-sharp ripostes, these performances reveal a shifting televisual landscape in which drag has both conformed to and contested the limits of its visibility.

AUSTRALIA AND AOTEAROA (NEW ZEALAND): INTERSECTIONAL AND INDIGENOUS

The development of drag on television in Australia and Aotearoa/ New Zealand has been uneven, emerging through national media systems shaped by the legacies of settler colonialism, localised cultural politics, and regionally specific aesthetics. Television is a medium closely tied to nation-building, and, in these contexts, this has both enabled the visibility of drag and revealed the limitations placed on its expression. Indeed, in one example, the *RuPaul's Drag Race Down Under* franchise has offered new visibility for performers, yet it has also been critiqued for failing to engage meaningfully with local histories, peoples, and diverse gender representation.

In Australia, early televised drag appeared largely as novelty acts in variety entertainment. Popular daytime shows, such as *The Mike Walsh Show* (1973–1985), featured a drag king performance from Jeanne Little. Little plays with gender non-conformity in her artistry. In 1984, Little performed *You and Me* alongside John-Michael Howson (National Film and Sound Archive of Australia n.d.). A decade later, drag exploded onto the big screens through mass visibility with the cinematic success of *The Adventures of Priscilla, Queen of the Desert* (1994). The legacy of this drag film is legendary, not only across Australia, but across the English-speaking world (more below). The popularity of *Priscilla* drew attention to the documentary *Ladies Please* (ABC, 1995), about the Sydney drag queens who inspired *Priscilla*, which profiled real-life queens like Cindy Pastel, Lady Bump, and others who worked the Oxford Street circuits. With a focus on visual and theatrical elements, this type of documentary often framed drag as flamboyant and entertainment, while not reflecting its political potency and creative community constructing capabilities.

While drag culture was notable in local cabaret circuits during the 1970s and 1980s in Aotearoa, particularly in cities like Wellington and Auckland, its visibility on mainstream television was extremely limited. Drag at that time was still viewed as part of a subcultural, queer-coded nightlife scene, and public broadcasters remained conservative and typically avoided explicitly queer content. Carmen Rupe, a pioneering Māori transgender performer and activist, broke this trend. In 1975, Rupe appeared on the television programme *Tonight at Nine*, where she discussed her life and experiences. This interview provided one of the very first examples of gender-diverse representation on New Zealand television during that era (Te Ara Encyclopedia of New Zealand n.d.). Similar to UK counterparts, shows like *A Week of It* (South Pacific Television, 1977–1979) or *McPhail & Gadsby* (1980–1985) included male comedians cross-dressing for comic effect, yet this was evidently played for laughs and had little to do with actual drag culture or queer identity.

House of Drag (TVNZ OnDemand, 2018–2020) popularised drag competitions in Aotearoa/New Zealand on TV before the arrival of *RuPaul's Drag Race Down Under*. This show pays attention to local, unique drag forms, showcasing artistry, personal narratives, and the creativity of contestants. *House of Drag* was hosted by renowned New Zealand drag queens Kita Mean and Anita Wigl'it, both of whom appeared in the first series of *RuPaul's Drag Race Down Under*. Notable here was the range of drag performances that moved beyond queens to include kings and non-binary artists. The show opened up the intersections of representation and norms within televised drag competitions. A Wellington-based drag king and trans man, Hugo Grrrl, won the first season, a small step in challenging the longstanding trend of a media focus on drag queens.

RuPaul's Drag Race Down Under arrived with all the glitter and franchise formula audiences have come to expect, showcasing Australasia's drag talent on the world stage. Despite its name, the show quickly drew criticism for its limited cultural awareness, raising old questions about what happens when global templates are dropped onto local scenes without fully reading the room. In one controversial example from the first season, one contestant provoked public pushback. Scarlett Adams was a contestant with a digital footprint revealing she had previously performed in blackface; Adams subsequently made a public apology (Boseley 2021). The issues of equity, diversity, and inclusion around *Drag Race* resurfaced, with viewers questioning how well the franchise understood the intersectional concerns of the communities it claimed to platform. Likewise, it revealed tensions within the drag community, prioritising commercialism over cultural awareness and respect.

The relationship between mainstream televised drag and local scenes is both dynamic and complicated. In Perth, for example, the work of Claire Alexander (2017) tracks how televised drag has sparked new creative energies, inspiring performers to play with style, format, and persona. Conversely, this focus on creativity ignites debates about authenticity, ownership, and the influence of marketable aesthetics. What gets platformed, and who gets left behind? These tensions are in no way unique to drag down under; they are part of the tensions created by the mainstreaming of drag for commercial reasons.

Television in Aotearoa has always been a complicated space, one where Māori and Indigenous cultures were often framed through a colonial lens: either romanticised, sanitised, or erased altogether. This is a trend that seems to be shifting, according to Jo Smith, who notes, 'Māori Television constitutes a significant political success by ensuring that Māori have a share in the mediascapes of New Zealand, and thus a share in particular economies of representation and expression' (2011: 721). The rise of Māori-led media has opened up room for storytelling that is relevant and accountable to communities. And drag, too, has started to reflect that shift, not just in terms of representation but also how drag carries and draws attention to the politics of specific contexts, concerns and communities. Season two of *RuPaul's Drag Race Down Under* addresses some of the concerns voiced by locals on reception of season one. Kween Kong expresses her Pasifika New Zealander identity, with Samoan and Tongan heritage, through costume, and story, layering her performances with ancestral presence. In speaking about her late sister, Madison, Kong says 'every time I get into drag, I always feel connected to her' (Koster 2024). Here, Kong is able to hold space for history, survival, and cultural continuity. Such drag is not simply entertainment; it is grounded in identity, culture, and politics.

Critique of class and the socio-economic politics of drag surface through the winner of season two of *RuPaul's Drag Race Down*

Under, as Spankie Jackzon offers DIY drag rooted in small-town Aotearoa. The view that her style was unpolished was a thread running through the series. Jackzon's style was shaped by her vast experience in regional performance circuits, and her wealth of entertainment more than compensated for her choice of wigs or rhinestones that were not always symmetrical. As drag has become highly merchandised, and the more polished looks are deemed more successful, there are socio-economic questions that linger around such 'success'. Jackzon's drag reveals something often hidden in drag – that representation of class is grounded in drag aesthetics and that drag can be expensive. Subverting these expectations is a timely reminder that drag has always been about resourcefulness, not just refinement.

Performance becomes political in terms of genderfluid representation, too. First seen by mainstream audiences on *Australian Idol* back in 2003, Courtney Act moved between drag and non-drag presentations in ways that unsettled the expectations of both. Act appeared in season six of the USA version of *Drag Race*. Later shows, like *The Bi Life* (E!, 2018) and *One Plus One* (ABC, 2021), gave her the space to hold complex conversations about gender, identity, and visibility, sharing her expertise by experience. Act's success and platform made queer fluidity legible on prime-time TV, a further step towards inclusion where visibility is a victory.

As is the case with representation across the continents, drag on TV in Australia and Aotearoa is shaped by what is commercially viable: palatable, market friendly, culturally neutral, and depoliticised. Yet, despite such sanitised constraints, performers demonstrate an ability to carve out critical spaces. Televised drag down under showcases drag that is playful and political, Indigenous and intersectional.

DRAG AND RADIO: SOUND VERSUS STAGE

Drag is undoubtedly a visual art, aesthetically and performatively. So, drag's relationship with sound is less often considered. In this section, we offer an overview of drag as an audio medium, on radio and in podcasting, where visibility is absent and voice and sound become the dominant site of performance. This shift in medium positions drag within new formats. Aesthetics such as wigs, garments, make-up, gesture, and stagecraft, give way to tone, pitch, accent, and rhythm. Here, sound is not simply a supporting element, but is the entire performance itself.

Radio, both historically and in contemporary digital formats, has long operated as a space for queer performance. For example, *Gaywaves* was one of the earliest queer radio programmes in Australia, broadcasting from 1979 on Sydney's 2SER-FM (see https://2ser.com/gaywaves). It was a groundbreaking show at a time when homosexuality was still criminalised in parts of Australia. At this time, when it was both risky and criminal to be visible, sound compensated and created a sense of community, because it was accessible to individuals from their own spaces. While radio historically limited visibility, it also enabled intimacy. One could listen alone. One could transmit queer voices anonymously, or receive them quietly, at home in private. That privacy becomes especially significant in contexts where queer and trans lives are surveilled or criminalised. Considering radio as a queer medium allows us to interrogate further how genders and sexualities are constructed and represented in media cultures, where the body is often assumed to be the primary site of focus. What forms of drag do we have when it is unseeable? What are the advantages and limitations of drag when it moves through airwaves instead of stages and screens?

One iconic drag radio performance can be found in British media archives: the musical comedy act of Hinge and Bracket. Performed by George Logan and Patrick Fyffe, their personas, Dr. Evadne Hinge and Dame Hilda Bracket, were mainstays of BBC Radio 4 in the late 1970s and early 1980s. They portrayed themselves as elderly, intellectual musicians. Their series, *The Random Jottings of Hinge and Bracket,* deployed arch humour, musical parody, and genteel innuendo to create a form of vocal drag that was both legible and palatable to mainstream audiences. It enabled a variation of drag that, precisely because it is disembodied, did not seem to provoke much discomfort. As well as a performance of gender disruption, they transmitted sounds of cultivated femininity crafted through vowel length, musical phrasing, and codified politeness through middle-class speech. Hinge and Bracket's queerness was ambient, never explicit, and yet fully saturated through their music and show. After initial success on the radio, they were known for later TV appearances.

Across Southeast Asia, drag and gender non-conformity have long circulated through informal and localised radio spaces, such as bakla radio DJs. In the Philippines, the term 'bakla' refers to individuals assigned male at birth who a feminine gender expression, often described as a distinct third gender in Filipino culture. Lloyd Cafe Cadena (1993–2020), affectionately known as 'Kween LC', was a prominent Filipino vlogger and radio personality. He gained popularity through his work as a radio DJ, and his shows were punctuated with storytelling and humour, resulting in YouTube success. Bakla radio DJs often broadcast in Taglish (a code-switched mix of Tagalog and English) and swardspeak (a uniquely Filipino queer slang). Bakla presenters construct on-air personas that blend advice-giving with innuendo-laden performance. Their voices are often high-pitched, theatrical, emotionally expressive, and intentionally effeminate (Garcia 2008). While not always identified as 'drag queens' in a Western sense, their on-air presence enacts many of the same performative strategies: parody, gendered exaggeration, and non-conformity to strict gender codes.

With the rise of podcasting in the 2000s, audio media entered a new phase. Once limited by frequency and geography, audio today can be subscribed to and streamed. Individuals can produce their own content and disseminate it rapidly; there is no shortage of outputs and there is much demand for more. In fact, as radio broadcasts may traditionally have sought to appeal to broad audiences, podcasting allows for specificity and multivocal forms.

One of the most prominent examples of drag podcasting is *Race Chaser*, hosted by former *RuPaul's Drag Race* contestants Alaska Thunderfuck and Willam Belli (Alaska & Willam 2021). While framed as an episode-by-episode review of the *Drag Race* franchise, the show frequently veers into industry critique, personal history, and unscripted gossip. Alaska's voice, in particular, is often known for its distinctive recognisability: pitched low, elongated, rich with performative drag, it is an example of how voice substitutes visibility.

Podcasting, then, creates new forms of auditory drag: less scripted, less stage-bound, but still structured. If radio in previous decades demanded legibility, through rigid standards that insisted on a certain cleanness of tone, podcasting allows for regional expression in terms of accents and expression. In podcasts, mistakes are kept in; conversation is key, rather than edited scripts.

Drag through sound has the ability to liberate the performance art. Since there are a number of visual economies that often discipline drag: race, size, age, ability, and other factors that shape how a body is read, audio opens up space for sonic identities that do not seek to conform. Of course, though, this should not be idealised: voice is still racialised, classed, and gendered. There is something archival about drag on the radio and in podcasts; these are both performances and histories in themselves. Drag's migration into audio shows its reframing: another way in which drag, ever adaptive, bends the medium to its own tune.

DRAG IN FILM: FROM DOCUMENTARY DRAG TO CINEMATIC CAMP

Drag has long been mediated by the screen. The following concise survey of films does not attempt to be exhaustive, but rather traces film archives through several key case studies, oscillating between documentary-type films and dramatic drag in cinematic performances. The differences are stark, and serve to highlight the distinction between the personal performer, and the performance itself.

One of the earliest drag documentaries appeared in 1969 in Britain, entitled *What's a Girl Like You …* It focussed on the London drag-scene, and took a behind-the-curtains look at the life of drag performers in London's Royal Vauxhall Tavern and in working-men's clubs in northern England. Here, the viewer can see regional differences in artistry, audience and reception. In terms of documenting the history of drag, the documentary is a rich social archive of British drag cultures. The film depicts interviews with performers who are open and candid about their lives and artistry, as well as their experiences of drag (BFI 1969).

Torch Song Trilogy (1988) represents a more muted and reflective account of drag. Harvey Fierstein plays the role of Arnold Beckoff, a Jewish drag performer. The film depicts Beckoff grappling with heartbreak, experiencing homophobia, and negotiating relationships with a mother who refuses to accept him. The film moves across years, tracing his shifting relationships, with lovers, with family, and with himself. Even as a film about drag, its drag scenes are sparse and unadorned; it prioritises presence over performance.

In the film, drag is represented with an emotional intimacy, including grief and memory. The reality of drag performance moves from fantasy and spectacle to autobiography in a film that is personal and authentic.

While not a specific film, the iconic drag character Divine cannot escape attention. The creation of Harris Glenn Milstead, Divine is one of the most transgressive and legacy-leaving figures in drag history. Divine gained popularity through co-creation with filmmaker John Waters, known for his irreverent, trashy and bizarre plots. Waters's work was punctuated by elements of both shock and camp, focussing on characters who are often outsiders and misfits. One of them can be seen in Divine's characters in films like *Pink Flamingos* (1972) and *Female Trouble* (1974) offer drag that is anarchic and often grotesque. In *Pink Flamingos*, for example, Divine's character picks up dog faeces and eats it. Glamour was not on Divine's agenda, but the tools of exaggeration were: big hair, heavy make-up, and outrageous costumes. Divine also played the role of Tracy Turnblad's mother, Edna, in John Waters's successful 1988 film *Hairspray*.

La Cage aux Folles (Molinaro 1978) draws on drag drama and theatricals. The film is set in Saint-Tropez and follows Albin and Renato, a middle-aged gay couple who run a drag nightclub. Albin's drag persona, Zaza, is central to the film. The narrative hinges on the couple's attempt to 'straighten up' when their son announces his engagement to the daughter of a far-right politician. The resulting chaos plays with queer in/visibility and concealment. While the film broke ground in its sympathetic portrayal of a long-term gay relationship, it simultaneously relied on camp excess to soften queerness for mainstream (heterosexual) consumption. Its success, both in Europe and in the USA, spawned remakes including *The Birdcage* (1996). *La Cage aux Folles* may celebrate queer domesticity, including the limited progress queer lives had made, yet the social tensions and taboos around drag remained in focus.

One of the most cited and contested documentaries within queer film history is Jennie Livingston's *Paris is Burning* (1990). Filmed in New York City in the late 1980s, it documents Black and Latinx performers within the ballroom scene, offering insights into drag and survival. The film's cultural impact is undisputed, yet its legacy remains ambivalent. In addition to performance and competitions, the ballroom is a space where individuals construct identity, affirm their genders and sexualities, and find belonging. Through competitive 'categories', contestants walk along the runway according to the theme. From military to high fashion, participants pursue and are scored on the 'realness' of these looks. The notion of families and houses is prominent in the film. Contestants compete from their chosen families led by house 'mothers' like Pepper LaBeija and Angie Xtravaganza. The mother is an experienced drag mentor, who provides care and support for their 'children', many of whom had been living precariously through familial rejection. Drag in ballroom culture is about community-making as well as competition.

While the film is unique in peeking behind the scenes at the lived realities of those in the documentary, bell hooks critiqued the film's gaze, arguing that Livingston's position as a white filmmaker problematises the ethics of its production and circulation. hooks writes:

> Had Livingston approached her subject with greater awareness of the way white supremacy shapes cultural production – determining not only what representations of blackness are deemed acceptable, marketable, as well as seeing – perhaps the film would not so easily have turned the black drag ball into a spectacle for the entertainment of those presumed to be on the outside of this experience looking in. So much of what is expressed in the film has to do with questions of power and privilege.
>
> (hooks 1992: 152)

To exemplify this point, one of the main queens in the film is Venus Xtravaganza, whose personal story reveals struggles of navigating sex work as a trans woman. She has aspirations for a better life, yet, by the end of the film, viewers learn she was murdered in an act of brutal transphobic violence. hooks observes that 'there is no mourning of him/her in the film, no intense sadness of this murder. Having served the purpose of "spectacle" the film abandons him/her … There are no scenes of grief. To put it crassly, her dying is upstaged by spectacle. Death is not entertaining' (hooks 1992: 154–155). hooks argues that the film presents the brutal murder without deep critical context, as the producers and editors do not offer critique of the structural forces (like transphobia, racism, and economic precarity) that contributed to her vulnerability. Therefore, hooks questions whether the film genuinely serves the interests of people like Venus, or if it instead provides a powerful emotional narrative for audiences to consume, without demanding political or material change. A recent documentary film, *I'm Your Venus* (2024), brings together Venus's two families – biological and ballroom – to focus on seeking answers to the unresolved case of her murder, and to celebrate her life. The film was directed by Kimberly Reed. Jennie Livingston, who directed *Paris Is Burning*, was one of the producers.

POSE (FX, 2018–2021) draws directly from *Paris is Burning*, engaging with the same culture, themes and experiences as the documentary. The fictional series explores the lives, relationships, and stories of Black and Latinx queer and trans communities within the same New York ballroom scene. As a longer series set in the same period, the representations of the ballroom scene benefit from being re-examined through contemporary eyes. *POSE* is able to expand the narrative, and explore the emotions and experiences through its characters' stories. Plots and narratives explore the challenges in characters' lives, including HIV/AIDS, poverty, homophobia and transphobia, and systemic racism. In terms of its community focus, the house system introduced in Livingston's film is central to *POSE*. Characters like Blanca Evangelista and Pray Tell illuminate the idea of drag families, as they support the emotional lifting of one another and their children. As *Paris is Burning* helped bring ballroom culture to wider attention and document the lives of those involved, *POSE* attempts to reframe that visibility; yet, this time with Black and Latinx queer and trans creatives behind the camera, reshaping how these stories are told. For example, among others, Janet Mock, a Black trans woman, served as a writer, director, and executive producer for the show.

In terms of film experience, *The Adventures of Priscilla, Queen of the Desert* (1994) offers high camp and flamboyance. In this way, it presents a different cinematic economy to documentary type films. The film depicts two drag queens, Mitzi and Felicia, and a trans woman, Bernadette, travelling through remote Australia in a bus lavishly named 'Priscilla'. They perform for bewildered locals, lip-sync to vast desert landscapes and endure homophobic and transphobic abuse in a number of bars, horrifically when their bus is graffitied with the term 'AIDS fuckers go home'.

Priscilla revels in costume and choreography; the film is undeniably visually iconic and this focus on spectacle has made its musical adaptation successful, too. For instance, there is an iconic scene where the main characters perform 'I Will Survive' by Gloria Gaynor in front of an Aboriginal camp; the audience seems to be enjoying the show through their clapping and dancing. The endurance of the song lyrics 'I Will Survive' alongside the presence of white drag in Aboriginal spaces cannot help but showcase the struggles and violence of colonial history. More than this, though, is that the Aboriginal characters are silent, as Pau Valera Rodríguez notes: 'Indigenous Australian men have been perpetually silenced and rarely appreciated as a subject with multiple potential identities' (Rodríguez 2012: 5). Problematically, then, Indigenous identity becomes a decorative backdrop. Similarly, the Filipina character, Cynthia, is introduced about halfway through the film, yet through the lenses of race, gender and postcolonial critiques, we see the character is steeped in racist and sexist stereotypes. She is portrayed as the mail-order bride of Bob, a mechanic who later becomes a lover to Bernadette. She is loud, hypersexual, drunk and, in one infamous scene, she pops ping-pong balls out of her vagina. Such a portrayal is entirely problematic, as Cynthia embodies a long history of racialised and misogynistic stereotypes about Asian women. Laforteza writes that 'Here, the Philippines and Filipinas are personified as a female/feminine body that is open for masculine white Australian conquest' (Laforteza 2006: 7). So, while *Priscilla* celebrates drag's flamboyance and its camp excess is unlimited, it does so through a framework that is built on damaging stereotypes of cultural difference. *Priscilla's* queerness is more performative than political.

A surface glance at drag films on screen reveals the prioritisation and popularity of queens in films, with low representation of drag kings and other flavours of drag. Yet, two films bring trans masculinities into focus: *By Hook or by Crook* (2001) and *Venus Boyz* (2002). *By Hook or by Crook* is a narrative feature film, co-directed by two trans men filmmakers. The story follows Shy, a small-time grifter who teams up with a neurodivergent trans man named Valentine. Though not explicitly 'drag' films, these films offer important explorations into gender performance as lived experience and survival that enable us to widen the vision of gender non-conformity on screen. There are no runways or sequins here: just worn hoodies, makeshift haircuts, and stolen moments of recognition. The film's refusal of cinematic gloss is precisely its strength; it insists on trans and queer lives as complex, messy, and non-spectacular.

With a more explicit focus on drag, Gabrielle Baur's documentary *Venus Boyz* (2002) directly addresses the performance of masculinity. Shot in both New York and Zurich, the film follows several AFAB performers and non-binary performers as they explore masculinity on stage. Unlike the polished pageantry of queen-centred films, *Venus Boyz* foregrounds the laborious construction of masculine personas. Binding, facial hair, and gesture are meticulously rehearsed. The film underscores that masculinity, no less than femininity, is a drag. As Del LaGrace Volcano, one of the film's protagonists, notes: 'I don't do male impersonation. I do masculinity in all its layered contradictions' (Skyy 2019).

More recently, Nicole Miyahara's *The Making of a King* (2015) documents the Los Angeles drag king community, exposing the privilege of queens in drag spaces, while performers navigate other intersectional identity markers such as gender, race, and class (Advocate Contributors 2016). Figures like Landon Cider and Havok Von Doom offer insights into the craft of kinging, including the idea of both creativity and risk at the core of their work. What is revealing about these documentary films is that identity is experienced and performed, and such films challenge what visibility in drag has historically looked like. Like all media forms, the film industry is shaped by race, class, gender, other politics of identity, and the shifting economies of representation.

DIGITAL DRAG

The internet became popular in the late 1990s, yet dial-up connections were expensive. By the mid-2000s, early social networks and forums saw the first flickers of digital drag culture thanks to broadband. On MySpace and GeoCities, performers shared grainy photos and flamboyant blog updates, connecting queer communities across time zones and global spaces. The turn of the twenty-first century saw the art of drag carefully feeling its way from the physical stage to the pixelated screen, laying the groundwork for the digital explosion to come.

As the 2000s unfolded, drag entered an era of digital and entrepreneurial opportunities. The rise of YouTube (2005), Facebook (2004), and later Instagram (2010) created direct channels for drag performers to reach global audiences without the need for bookings, club promoters, or TV networks. Access was easier. Certain performers became 'drag influencers', generating hundreds of thousands of followers with viral make-up tutorials, comedy skits, and lip-sync videos. By the late 2010s, it was common to distinguish between 'stage kings/queens' and 'social media kings/queens', the latter sometimes achieving fame entirely online before ever setting foot on a nightclub stage (Feldman & Hakim 2020).

The drag economy expanded in the following key directions:

- **Paid streaming performances:** Especially during crises like the Covid pandemic, drag performers learned to monetise live streams. Platforms like StageIt and Twitch enabled ticketed digital shows where fans around the world paid for and viewed performances in real time. A simple ring light and webcam could transform a domestic space into a show space, allowing drag performers to keep earning even when physical venues shut down.
- **Merchandise and branding:** Successful drag artists launched merchandise empires. It became common for a popular performer to sell their brands via T-shirts, enamel pins of their catchphrases, or even custom make-up palettes. This commercialisation was a significant change in the amount of income drag could generate.
- **Crowdfunding and fan patronage:** The advent of Patreon and OnlyFans provided new avenues for income. Many performers set up monthly subscriptions where superfans could fund their creative projects in exchange for exclusive content. On OnlyFans (a platform originally known for adult content but also used by artists), numerous drag stars found a paying audience for behind-the-scenes videos, uncensored looks, or even out-of-drag modelling. During the pandemic lockdowns, OnlyFans 'helped many drag artists … make a living' (Sim 2025). By venturing into these spaces, drag artists demonstrated commercial and economic strategic thinking, as well as performance artistry.

- **Mainstream media and cameos:** With drag's surge in popularity, performers began appearing in films, TV commercials,
talk shows, and music videos, often for substantial fees. This
diversification meant that by the mid-2010s, 'Drag is not a
hobby, it's a career', as queen Latrice Royale famously declared
(Feldman & Hakim 2020).

Underpinning this new economy was the power of social media.
A polished Instagram feed or a political or witty Twitter presence
became a platform for self-promotion and branding for rising per-
fomers. The most followed drag artists racked up staggering numbers of followers; for example, Brazil's Pabllo Vittar amassed over 11
million Instagram followers and became known as 'the world's most
popular drag queen', eclipsing even RuPaul in social media reach
(Schlutt 2020). *Drag Race* alumna Jasmine Masters put it plainly:
once you achieve fame on a platform, 'you are a brand … you have
to treat yourself as a market, as a business' (Feldman & Hakim 2020).

With the rise of social media platforms, drag performance has
entered new spaces to be able to transform the art. These platforms
also create communities between followers/fans and performers,
and support networks between performers. Aesthetics and algorithms combine in digital drag, and as Bragança and Ostruca note
in their research on Brazilian drag, 'YouTube can be viewed as a
space in which issues of gender, race and sexuality, among other
issues related to underrepresentation are freely voiced' (Bragança &
Ostruca 2023: 131). They note how the popularity of the platform
has been particularly embraced by young drag queens, indicative of
the popularity of *RuPaul's Drag Race*.

Arti Sandhu's article 'India's Digital Drag Aunties' (2019) explores
how drag culture uses Indian dress and costumes with activist intent
to challenge heteronormative ideas, and to represent issues related to
LGBTQ+ individuals. Sandhu's analysis focuses on two drag queens
popularised by social media: Maya the Drag Queen (performed by
Alex Mathew) and Pammi Aunty (performed by Ssumier Pasricha).
Sandhu notices the breakaway from Western ideas of drag in favour
of embracing national aesthetics. These two performers represent
the figure of the 'aunty', an older respected woman in Indian and
South Asian communities. The representation is through the use
of fashion, as Sandhu says: 'Through parodying familiar familial

structures and gender stereotypes such as the Punjabi aunty or Kerala housewife the intention of Indian drag queens is to challenge and resist these gendered and wider patriarchal frameworks' (Sandhu 2019: 72). While embracing traditional dress, the use of the digital platform is entirely contemporary. Their use of platforms like Facebook and YouTube generates visibility and a community for those who access drag from their own, often safer, locations.

Digital platforms in Japan (YouTube, TikTok, Nico Nico Douga – a Japanese video-sharing site, and other cosplay platforms) have popularised performers who engage with 'cross-dressing' (*josō*), cosplay, and *otokonoko* culture. Otokonoko culture is shaped around men or boys in Japan who dress and present themselves in a traditionally 'feminine' way for performative and entertainment purposes. To call this drag would be an incorrect appropriation and assimilation, but there is an obvious connection. Otokonoko performers use similar techniques: make-up transformation, wigs, costume, and character performance. On YouTube, performers like *Ichika* present exaggerated feminine personas through make-up tutorials and vlogs. On Nico Nico Douga, users can retain their anonymity and engage in live performances and streams. In cosplay, digital platform users can take on costume, dress, and styles similar to anime characters, blending drag with fan performance. Yet digital drag in Japan is not really radical or politically motivated. As an entertainment form, it focuses on transformation, fantasy, and aesthetics. The visual is the primary focus, and a number of performances do not use speech. Japan's broader media culture often has popularised gender play through anime or manga, for example, but this is not always labelled as queer. Sharon Kinsella observes, 'In twenty-first century Japan, male cross-dressing (josō) has become a popular element of culture at multiple levels, from the most convivial and grass roots amateur and fan participation to mass media entertainment' (Kinsella 2020: 40).

While drag queens have long dominated drag on TV and in film, discussed earlier, the surge in online performance during the 2020s has created new opportunities for drag kings to represent their forms online. Historically underrepresented in mainstream drag coverage, kings have increasingly used digital platforms to push against the hyper-femme, reality-TV drag model popularised by *RuPaul's Drag Race*. Their performances are often hybridised with cabaret, punk, cosplay, and experimental video and bring a different aesthetic to online drag: less sparkle, more stubble! Drag kings have turned to platforms like *Instagram Live*, *Twitch*, and *Vimeo* to build followings. The COVID pandemic and enforced lockdowns meant a number of performers were unable to work in their normal venues, and therefore, they embraced digital opportunities to maintain their artistry and audiences. *Kings of the World* (*KOTW*) was launched during the pandemic as a monthly digital drag king variety show streamed on Twitch. International in scope and representation, *KOTW* was produced by drag kings Johnny Gentleman, Pelvis Breastly, and Mo B. Dick, and was able to mobilise the proximity afforded by digital spaces in order to platform artists from a range of continents, fostering a unique digital community (Kings Of The World 2020). LoUis CYfer, a UK drag king, moved online to participate in virtual cabaret performances and digital events. During an interview about the impact of the pandemic, CYfer discusses the variety of opportunities embraced in the digital sphere: 'I've gone digital baby!!! This includes working with my own avatar as a way to explore character and technology. I've started my own podcast' (Andro & Eve 2020).

It is not just digital platforms that are able to move drag from physical to digital spaces. The arrival of artificial intelligence (AI) can change the form entirely. The future of drag performance will undoubtedly be shaped by cutting-edge technology as new mediums of expression. The art of drag has always been about transformation and illusion, and now those qualities are finding fertile ground in AI, virtual reality (VR), and augmented reality (AR). The period from 2015 to 2025 has seen drag artists experiment with technology in ways that blur the line between the physical and the digital, creating new forms of performance. One pioneering example is drag in virtual reality. In 2022, an experimental show called *Queens of the Metaverse* in London featured drag performers debuting looks that were designed using VR and AR technologies. Facebook's parent company Meta publicised this as the 'first-ever mixed reality drag show', highlighting how tech companies see drag artists as ideal collaborators for demonstrating new technology, quite simply as they embrace progress through creativity (Meta 2022).

Make-up and costumes, some of the essential ingredients of drag, also benefit from tech infusion. 3D-printed costumes and prosthetics help create avant-garde looks that were once impossible to construct by hand. Digital fashion, where a performer wears a green screen bodysuit and the outfit is placed on them via computer graphics, can been used in digital drag videos. Some drag artists have toyed with AI image generators to brainstorm looks or even project AI-generated backgrounds during shows.

Crucially, drag is also influencing technology. Technologists working with drag performers have had to make their algorithms more robust. After all, a drag face with extreme make-up can confuse facial recognition tech, and drag artists have gleefully noted that in a world of increasing surveillance, a good drag face is practically anti-facial-recognition camouflage! In a sense, drag is queering technology, asking it to bend and not be so binary. Joe Parslow has pioneered research into this emerging area in his article, 'Kings, Queens, Monsters, and Things: Digital Drag Performance and Queer Moves in Artificial Intelligence (AI)' (2023). Parslow examines drag AI by using the case study of *The Zizi Project*. *The Zizi Project* (https://zizi.ai) centres on art and performance pieces created by artist Jake Elwes in collaboration with Me The Drag Queen and members of London's drag performance scene. *The Zizi Project* includes three works: *Queering the Dataset*, *Zizi & Me*, and *The Zizi Show*. In *Queering the Dataset*, Elwes inserted 1,000 images of drag performers into a facial recognition programme to reproduce them using AI. Yet, rather than look for realistic reproductions, the work embraces failure, as the outputs expose the faults with the technology. In *Zizi & Me*, a video performance was created with Me The Drag Queen. Elwes used footage of Me to produce a deepfake version of her, and the performance was a duet between the live performer and her digital double. Yet, there were glitches, where the AI was unsuccessful in representing face or gesture. *The Zizi Show* extended this work into an interactive cabaret, showcasing 13 deepfake versions of drag performers. Audiences could switch between acts and artists. The arrival and advancement of AI has the capacity to expose, disrupt, and reimagine drag, raising questions of ownership, authenticity and ethics, as Parslow states:

> something more exciting occurs as new horizons of queerly digital performance practices begin to emerge. These utopian considerations frame *The Zizi Project* as laden with potentiality for queer performance futures, where drag and AI interact

and intersect in complex ways to sketch out new possibilities for queer performance.

(Parslow 2023: 129)

In addressing the ethical anxieties surrounding AI, Parslow cites *The Zizi Project* as an example that complicates, rather than replicates, AI function. In brief, AI invites a reconsideration of what counts as performance, identity, and even drag. The role of AI in drag is nascent and emerging, and an area which will undoubtedly transform the art form in coming years.

Digital drag presents benefits and contradictions. Access, accessibility, representation, safety, community, and even anonymity mean drag is accessible from almost any location, on any device across the globe. Yet the use of AI technology, specifically in relation to deepfake content, raises ethical questions around content, ownership, and economic concerns about pay. Digital drag spaces are orientated around community, care, and collaboration. Performers and audiences can interact through live events, using comment sections, emoji responses and even making donations. Nonetheless, this must come with a warning. In terms of technology, research shows how algorithms do not have neutrality, and there is bias in how they reward certain kinds of content: short, visually striking, often conforming to Eurocentric beauty norms (Trammel 2023). In her research on digital drag queens on TikTok specifically, Krysten Stein's (2023) analysis of 50 drag videos with over 40,000 likes concludes how white femme drag is the most visible of drag online. Here, the representation of drag is still inequitable; the algorithms function as a new kind of gatekeeping governed by metrics and monetisation.

DRAG AND MERCHANDISE

Commercialisation is the process where cultural practices, products, or identities are transformed into marketable goods or services for the purposes of profit. For drag specifically, commercialisation in the media age has been central to the growth of its industry. Laamanen et al. discuss how 'the contemporary drag marketplace represents a multi-million dollar industry that reaches far beyond traditional queer venues and audiences' (2025: 1). As drag has moved from bars and basements into studios, shopping centres and sponsored livestreams, it has become a site of branding, merchandising, and monetised visibility. For critics and activists, there is now a growing unease, and this gold rush has raised questions: has drag sold out? At what cost to drag's radical spirit? As more money flowed in, fear arose that the art was losing its edge.

RuPaul's Drag Race, a franchise of global proportions, is the perfect example of this. Beyond the on-screen show, there are product lines, tours, cosmetics, podcasts, merchandise, conventions, and brand endorsements. Fans can buy RuPaul's music, Trixie Mattel make-up, Jinkx Monsoon tea towels. Luigi Squillante (2025) notes how 'the Ru-niverse' has had successful collaborations with mainstream commercial brands and sponsorship of international events. It would be erroneous to conceive this as a new trend. The performance industry has always been invested in profit generation, in order to pay artists, venues and maintain standards. There is a unique distinction between UK and USA drag, for example, in which the former is paid by the venue owners for the performance, while in the USA, drag artists seek tips from audience members to support their income. Throughout the industry, there are examples of deliberate exploitation, where artists are not appropriately remunerated for their work, being asked to work for 'exposure' rather than payment. There is a cost to visibility.

The global model privileges certain kinds of drag. As noted earlier, the algorithms on social media sites privilege performers who are polished, marketable, and aligned with dominant beauty standards; these artists tend to benefit most. Squillante observes how '"neoliberal drag" has higher chances to foster acceptance and recognition of queer inputs within the mainstream culture' (2025: 25). Here, the drag industry is prioritised over its art forms. These cultures are embedded with a politics of visibility in relation to race, gender, and body norms. Drag queens of colour, including Heidi N Closet, Mariah Balenciaga, Latrice Royale, Mayhem Miller, Widow Von'Du, and The Vixen have all documented the racism embedded in public responses and industry treatment, particularly from 'fans' (Reynolds 2020; Menchavez 2020). The idea of drag as a business has also led to an emphasis on aesthetics that undoubtedly gives more exposure to drag queens, as Stein (2023) notes earlier. Drag kings, non-binary performers and other performers whose drag is gritty, gender-divergent, or regional may struggle to find the same success.

The pink pound plays a central role. Coined in the UK, the term 'pink pound' refers to the spending power of the LGBTQ+ community. In media and advertising, the queer community is used as a demographic category to be targeted with tailored products. Drag is often used to front these campaigns. For example, in the UK, the pharmacy and beauty products chain, Superdrug, featured performances by drag queens at events in Manchester and Brighton. This advertising campaign included the 'Superdrag Lip-Sync', with the aim of raising funds for LGBTQ+ helplines (Superdrug n.d.).

'Pinkwashing' or 'rainbow capitalism' are terms used to describe the strategic use of LGBTQ+ symbols, identities, or causes, particularly rainbow imagery and Pride campaigns. Their use by corporations, governments, or organisations to present themselves as progressive or inclusive often obscures unethical practices or lack of meaningful support for LGBTQ+ communities. This is similar to 'greenwashing' with regards to environmental concerns. Critics of 'pinkwashing' observe how this inclusion is seasonal, often peaking during Pride month, and rarely extends into long-term support (Holmes 2022).

In this way, commercial dynamics point to tensions around the function and impact of drag in the media age: radical artistry or commercial commodification? Undoubtedly, the commercialisation of drag has increased its visibility and raised the profile of a number of performers. In exchange, this often results in the platforming and privileging of certain drag forms: white drag queens. If drag is a queer art form, how far does its mainstream assimilation dilute its in-your-face political queerness?

DRAG AND MUSIC

Music has long been a staple feature of drag's history. As noted in Chapter 1, in early twentieth-century vaudeville and music hall, male and female impersonators performed comic and romantic numbers, using music to build character and draw attention to the performance of gender itself. Performers like Vesta Tilley and Julian Eltinge sang, mimed, and subverted gender through music. From lip-syncs and live vocals to DJ sets, mashups and musical parodies, music is a key ingredient to drag performance. In digital drag spaces, musical diversity expands further. Performers on platforms like TikTok or Instagram often use stitched audio, mixing pop, spoken word, soundbites from film and TV, and political speeches. In this sense, drag performance becomes a collage of sound, commonly known as 'mash ups'.

A number of drag musicians, like Pabllo Vittar and Trixie Mattel, write and perform original songs, gaining followings not only as drag performers but as musicians in their own right. Here, music moves from background to authorship. In drag queen performance culture, especially in Anglophone contexts, music performances pay homage to pop and disco divas: Judy Garland, Beyoncé, Gloria Gaynor, Tina Turner, Cher, Liza Minnelli. The popularity of these performances is due to the emotions entwined in the music. Yet this focus on diva anthems obscures the broader repertoire of drag. Drag kings, for instance, often draw from rock, hip-hop, country, or indie music to construct masculinities. A king performing Freddie Mercury or Elvis Presley may emphasise swagger and exaggerate sexualised energies through hip thrusts. Others might lip-sync to artists like Lil Nas X, Prince, or Tyler, the Creator, where masculinity is already unstable and performative. Landon Cider's winning performance on *Dragula* (season three, 2019) famously fused punk, horror, and theatricality, challenging the assumption that drag must be femme, glossy, or polished (Fandom n.d.).

Still, lip-syncing remains drag's most recognisable musical form, but it comes with its own critiques of not being 'real' music or performance. Stephen Farrier takes this as his point of reflection in questioning the place of lip-syncing in drag. He states, 'given that drag queens are often known for their quick acidic wit, it is puzzling why many of them give so much stage time to other people's voices through lip-synching' (Farrier 2016: 192). Farrier challenges the notion that drag queens' use of other people's voices through lip-syncing equates to a lack of originality or talent. Instead, he argues that lip-synching is a different form of talent. Using other's music creates a lineage, a cultural memory, a queer connection. Farrier states, 'By definition, the material that a drag queen lip-synchs to is always recorded in the past... This pastness makes a connection to histories that the community sees as important' (2016: 197). Farrier illuminates this point by placing emphasis on the technicality, precision and training of lip-syncing in the drag performer Meth. He draws attention to aspects such as vocal breath, vibrato, the physical punctuation of lyrics, all of which demonstrate a rich performance awareness in itself. For Farrier (2016), lip-syncing is a means of 'digging the past', an act of remembering, tributing and paying homage to cultural legacies.

Indeed, lip-syncing has been noted by Finn Lefevre as problematic in terms of how it has been used in *RuPaul's Drag Race*. Rather than be a mode of self-expression and defiance in drag, for queer artists and trans people, the lip-sync has become combative, and signals battle. Lefevre states, 'What was once a favorite method of self-declaration, defiance and identity exploration for trans people now often feels exclusionary. While RuPaul asks contestants to "lip sync for their lives" we are literally fighting for ours' (2021: 249–250).

Music extends beyond background noise in drag; it transmits identity. Whether synced, sung, or silent, music is a medium through which drag has voice.

DRAG AND LIVE ART: THE POLITICS OF THE BODY

Live art is a form of experimental performance that uses the body to explore and project creative ideas, often outside traditional theatre or gallery settings. Live art can include multi-media performances, photography, installations, and fine art. From the mid-1970s into the 1980s, the punk scene influenced live art through its rejection of commercialism by using raw music, DIY aesthetics, and anti-establishment politics. At the intersection with live art, drag becomes a conceptual tool, a political gesture, and a provocation. Here, drag is not concerned with gender impersonation or runway looks; it functions as a method and process for creating art. This section offers a short selection of live artists who operate within the remit of experimental gender non-conformity or drag. As will be seen, live art challenges dominant drag aesthetics and opens up new terrains of queer expression.

The Cockettes were a radical and experimental theatre troupe. They began in San Francisco in the late 1960s and early 1970s as part of a counter-cultural movement. They were known for their gender-bending performances and extravagant drag, and their aesthetics went beyond gender impersonation to include both androgyny and nudity. The Cockettes had radical views about performance creation and art that sought to disrupt established theatre methods. They made adaptations of films and musicals, including a re-imagining of *The Wizard of Oz*, using psychedelics and a gender-bending twist. This still influences some contemporary adaptations (Kruger n.d.). Some of the notable individuals involved in the Cockettes included Sylvester, a drag performer and singer who later became a famous disco artist. While only active for a short period, the Cockettes had a profound influence on drag culture, experimental film and musicals, performance art, and LGBTQ+ visibility.

This experimental ethos continued in London's 1980s club scene and is often epitomised through Leigh Bowery. In collaboration with choreographer Michael Clark, Bowery's performances were extravagant, grotesque, and deliberately unreadable. Bowery used prosthetics, full-body suits, sculptured costuming, and paint. His drag went beyond gender. Bowery's looks often refused gender legibility as he played with horror, glamour, and excess. In making himself unrecognisable, Bowery disrupted the visual economy of both fashion and gender performance. Bowery was painted naked by renowned artist, Lucien Freud and his life is documented by his closest friend, Sue Tilley, in the biography, *Leigh Bowery: The Life and Times of an Icon* (1997).

Across the Atlantic, Vaginal Davis similarly defies categorisation and unsettles social norms. Davis emerged from the queer punk scenes of 1980s Los Angeles. For Davis, drag is anarchic; she engages with DIY-drag, performance lectures, and racial politics. Her personas are often caricatures of whiteness, respectability, or femininity, and therefore sit at the intersections of race, gender, and class. Davis's drag is an ongoing site of disruption, where creativity, improvisation, and refusal are key ingredients. In contrast to dominant drag narratives today, her work defies the commercial sanitisation of drag and insists on its subversive potential.

As a live performance artist, Ethyl Eichelberger peaked in popularity also peaked during the 1980s and was known for his incredible ability in drag. Eichelberger often took on personas of strong, mythological women. As a profilic playwright and classically trained actor, Eichelberger cared about inhabiting the character deeply and performing with exaggerated and sometimes surreal theatricality.

Eichelberger's drag was clearly influenced by his involvement with Charles Ludlam's *Ridiculous Theatrical Company*. The company was famous for its over-the-top performances. Eichelberger was an accomplished musician, often bringing live music into his drag performances. Eichelberger's drag was also a physical performance, using acrobatic skills, fire-eating, and musical performances. Eichelberger appeared in the HBO series *Encyclopedia* (1988).

This commitment to theatrical embodiment would continue into the 1990s with British performer, David Hoyle, whose chaotic stage presence brought raw politics into the heart of queer performance. Hoyle rose to prominence in the 1990s, formerly known as *The Divine David* on Channel 4 in the UK. He works at the edge of drag, cabaret, and performance art. Hoyle's shows often collapse in on themselves, described as chaotic, emotional, and politically charged. His persona is camp, but not safe: he offers powerful critiques of nationalism, neoliberalism, and queer assimilation. Hoyle connects with audiences as part of his performance, thereby rejecting the safe space of passive spectatorship. He uses performance as a form of live confrontation open to inspiration, spontaneity, and failure. Hoyle's live art drag is demanding, unstable, and emotionally raw. Hoyle also features in the 2021 musical drama, *Everybody's Talking About Jamie*, a film that narrates the events of a student who has aspirations of becoming a drag queen.

Excessive durational performances are a popular form of live art, and Taylor Mac's *A 24-Decade History of Popular Music* (2016) is a primary example of this. The performance lasted 24 hours and spanned 240 years of American history with over 246 songs. Mac's objective was to examine US history through a queer lens, and the performance premiered at St. Ann's Warehouse in Brooklyn. Mac's drag was excessive and theatrical, and the audience often participated as co-performers.

Like Mac, Cassils challenges perceptions of the body through physical art. Cassils, a transmasculine, non-binary performance artist, uses the language of bodybuilding, endurance, and violence to interrogate the visibility and power of masculinities. In their work *Becoming an Image* (2012), performed in darkness and lit only by camera flash, Cassils destabilises binary readings of the body, gender, and spectacle. While not always framed as drag, their manipulation of gender aesthetics aligns with the critical functions of drag-as-performance. Drag is iconically arresting and has been captured by numerous photographers and exhibitions that bear testament to its artistry.

This sketch of drag and live performance art centres the harmonious marriage of both art forms, characterised by their shared rebellious ethos, refusal to assimilate, and a deep political engagement. Live art is punctuated by its anarchy and resistance to rules. It is therefore unsurprising that drag is a popular art form, used to destabilise normative ideas of gender, performance, and spectatorship. The rawness of live art contrasts sharply with audience expectations of performance that is rehearsed and polished. Live art privileges process and risk, seeking to embrace the unexpected. Such performances remain countercultural and are not considered mainstream; their lack of structure is often aligned to failure. Yet, such failure is productive; as Jack Halberstam (2011) argues, queer failure can resist dominant scripts of success and respectability.

CONCLUSION

The earlier parts of the chapter traced drag's movements through historical moments in television, film, and radio. Here, representation was restricted, and 'decency' meant drag was palatable to audiences. Even the most seemingly harmless sketches, sitcoms, or variety turns had the potential to reveal deeper cultural anxieties about gender, class, and sexuality. Drag may have been made legible on TV, but rarely on its own terms.

RuPaul's Drag Race changed the scale and economics of drag on screen. Its global reach and impact on drag is indisputable, and its influence stretches far beyond the screen. *Drag Race's* success sits in tension with queerness. While it brings visibility, it also brings standardisation and commodification. It celebrates queerness while also making it a specific, structured, and formulaic form for mainstream audiences. Many performers exist outside this economy entirely and actively resist it. Drag certainly extends beyond competition formats or monetisable content, and this does not make these forms any less valuable. Indeed, we argue, quite the opposite.

Digital drag, in its multiplicity, demonstrates the ongoing resilience and creativity of the form. The Covid pandemic shifted drag onto screens out of necessity, and this also permitted the creation of new spaces of connection, care, and critique. Of course, users must remain critical to algorithms that retain and mirror the same cultural biases that makes mainstream drag 'successful'.

Commercialisation has intensified all of these tensions. Whether through merchandise, brand deals, or Pride campaigns, drag is now entangled in global marketing strategies. It is not inherently wrong that drag is profitable for some; artists deserve decent pay. But the terms of such profitability raise significant questions. Is drag diluted by its mainstream reach? Who benefits when queerness becomes a seasonal aesthetic for corporate campaigns? The question is not whether drag should be commercial, but whether it can remain critical and political when it is. Drag cannot be reduced to a singular media narrative or easy slogans, nor restricted by dominant formats. Its vitality lies in its evasion of fixed identity and formats. Difference and diversity in drag are non-negotiable.

FURTHER READING

Brennan, N. & Gudelunas, D. (eds). (2022). *Drag in the Global Digital Public Sphere: Queer Visibility, Online Discourse and Political Change.* **Abingdon: Routledge.** This edited collection explores how drag performers use digital platforms around the world, with an explicit focus away from *RuPaul's Drag Race*. The collection of essays detail global examples from Brazil, South Africa, the Philippines, and beyond. The case studies detail representations of kings, monsters, and non-binary expressions.

DeCaro, F. (2019). *Drag: Combing Through the Big Wigs of Show Business.* **New York: Rizzoli.** A glossy, illustrated chronicle of drag and its presence in entertainment industries. In this accessible account, DeCaro narrates profiles of key performers from vaudeville to *RuPaul's Drag Race*.

Ginibre, J.-L. (2005). *Ladies or Gentlemen: A Pictorial History of Male Cross-Dressing in the Movies.* **New York: Filipacchi Publishing.** A visually rich photographic archive of male cross-dressing in Hollywood and international cinema.

McGlotten, S. (2021). *Dragging: Or, In the Drag of a Queer Life.* **Abingdon: Routledge.** An ethnographic exploration of drag as performance and identity. McGlotten merges personal narrative with analysis of culture to investigate how drag intersects with race and technology across physical and digital spaces.

Mercer, J., Sarson, C., & Hakim, J. (eds). (2023). *RuPaul's Drag Race and the Cultural Politics of Fame.* **Abingdon: Routledge.** This volume interrogates RuPaul's global media empire. Essay contributions offer both celebratory and critical perspectives on the cultural impact of *Drag Race*.

Russo, V. (1981). *The Celluloid Closet: Homosexuality in the Movies*. New York: Harper & Row. A groundbreaking early study of queer representation in film, including drag and coded forms of same-sex expressions.

Suárez, J. A. (1996). *Bike Boys, Drag Queens, and Superstars: Avant-Garde, Mass Culture, and Gay Identities in the 1960s Underground Cinema*. Bloomington, IN: Indiana University Press. Focusing on queer and drag-infused experimental film in 1960s New York, Suárez explores how underground cinema became a space for contesting sexual norms and mainstream media.

GLOSSARY

Algorithmic online performance   The rules and outcomes of digital platforms, shaped by what the algorithm chooses to show based on its knowledge of user profiles and popularity of sources.

Commercialisation   The process of enterprise or activity for financial gain.

Confessional   In reality TV, a direct-to-camera moment where a performer narrates thoughts, reactions or gossip behind the scenes.

Cosplay   Dressing as a character from a cartoon, film, book, or video game.

Deepfake   A video of a person where voice or facial expressions have been altered; often used maliciously or to spread false information.

Drag family   A chosen network of support in drag, where performers take on roles like mothers, daughters, or siblings.

Encoding/decoding   In Stuart Hall's theory, a way of understanding media where creators intend to produce meaning, but viewers might read it differently based on their own contexts.

Facial recognition technology   Software that scans faces for privacy and security purposes.

House   In ball culture, a family unit of drag performers who compete, create, and care for each other like family.

Josō   In Japanese, the act of cross-dressing (usually male to female); it translates as 'women's clothing'.

Lip-sync   Mouthing the words to a song in performance.

Mainstream   Widely accepted as popular, designed to appeal to the masses.

Merch   Merchandise, i.e. goods and accessories that turn a performer's brand into something fans can buy.

Neoliberal drag   Drag made to fit into commercial culture: market-friendly, brandable, and polished.

Palatability   How easy something is for the general public to accept.

Persona   The character or identity a performer creates for the stage or screen.

Podcasting Producing audio-based content for digital distribution.

Postcolonial critique A critical approach that examines the lasting effects of colonialism and imperialism on various aspects of society and culture.

Representation The way people and communities are shown, or left out, in media and popular culture.

Reality TV Live, supposedly unscripted shows that are then edited.

Subversive Something that disrupts norms, rules or expectations.

Swardspeak A playful, coded mix of Filipino, English, and queer slang used in LGBTQ+ circles in the Philippines.

Visibility politics Who gets seen, how people are represented, and its relationships to power and inclusion.

REFERENCES

Advocate Contributors (2016). 'Let "The Making of a King" Introduce You to the World of Drag Kings'. Advocate. Retrieved from www.advocate.com/transgender/2016/9/27/let-making-king-introduce-you-world-drag-kings-video (accessed June 2025).

Alaska & Willam (2021). 'Race Chaser: A Drag Race Podcast with Alaska & Willam'. Retrieved from https://foreverdogpodcasts.com/podcasts/race-chaser (accessed June 2025).

Alexander, C. (2017). 'What Can Drag Do for Me? The Multifaceted Influences of *RuPaul's Drag Race* on the Perth Drag Scene'. In Brennan, N. & Gudelunas, D. (eds), *RuPaul's Drag Race and the Shifting Visibility of Drag Culture: The Boundaries of Reality TV*, 245–269. Basingstoke: Palgrave Macmillan.

Andro & Eve (2020). 'Let's Meet LoUis CYfer!' Retrieved from https://androandeve.com/lets-meet-louis-cyfer (accessed June 2025).

BBC News. (2019). 'Barry Humphries: Top Comedy Prize Renamed after Transgender Row'. Retrieved from www.bbc.co.uk/news/world-australia-47943745 (accessed June 2025).

BFI. (1969). 'What's a Girl Like You…' Retrieved from https://player.bfi.org.uk/free/film/watch-whats-a-girl-like-you-1969-online (accessed June 2025).

Boseley, M. (2021). 'RuPaul's Drag Race Down Under Contestant Apologises for Past Performances in Blackface'. *The Guardian*. Retrieved from www.theguardian.com/tv-and-radio/2021/mar/18/rupauls-drag-race-down-under-contestant-apologises-for-past-performances-in-blackface (accessed June 2025).

Bragança, L., & Ostruca, D. (2023). 'Werq the YouTube: Changing Collective Practices in the Brazilian Drag Scene'. In Brennan, N. & Gudelunas, B. (eds), *Drag in the Global Digital Public Sphere*, 126–139. Abingdon: Routledge.

Brennan, N., & Gudelunas, D. (2017). *RuPaul's Drag Race and the Shifting Visibility of Drag Culture*. Basingstoke: Palgrave Macmillan.

CBC Arts. (n.d.). 'Canada's A Drag'. Retrieved from https://gem.cbc.ca/media/canadas-a-drag (accessed June 2025).

Fandom. (n.d.). 'The Boulet Brothers' Dragula (Season 3)'. RuPaul's Drag Race Wiki. Retrieved from https://rupaulsdragrace.fandom.com/wiki/The_Boulet_Brothers%27_Dragula_(Season_3) (accessed June 2025).

Farrier, S. (2016). 'That Lip-Synching Feeling: Drag Performance as Digging the Past'. In Campbell, A. & Farrier, S. (eds), *Queer Dramaturgies: International Perspectives on Where Performance Leads Queer* 192–209. Basingstoke: Palgrave Macmillan.

Feldman, Z. & Hakim, J. (2020). 'RuPaul's Drag Race: How Social Media Made Drag's Subversive Art Form into a Capitalist Money Maker'. Retrieved from www.kcl.ac.uk/rupauls-drag-race-how-social-media-made-drags-subversive-art-form-into-a-capitalist-money-maker (accessed June 2025).

Garcia, J. N. C. (2008). *Philippine Gay Culture: Binabae to Bakla, Silahis to MSM*. Hong Kong: Hong Kong University Press.

Halberstam, J. (2011). *The Queer Art of Failure*. Durham, NC: Duke University Press.

Hall, S. (1980). 'Encoding/Decoding'. In Hall, S., Hobson, D., Lowe, A., & Willis, P. (eds), *Culture, Media, Language*, 128–138. Abingdon: Routledge.

Hayward, A. (2018). 'Danny La Rue: Female Impersonator Who Made Drag into an Art Form'. *The Independent*. Retrieved from www.the-independent.com/news/lifeinfocus/danny-la-rue-death-anniversary-obituary-drag-queen-cabaret-hello-dolly-a8934691.html (accessed June 2025).

Holmes, A. (2022). 'Resisting Pinkwashing: Adaptive Queerness in Vancouver Pride Parades'. In Blidon, M. & Brunn, S. D. (eds), *Mapping LGBTQ Spaces and Places*, 445–463. Cham: Springer.

hooks, b. (1992). *Black Looks: Race and Representation*. Boston, MA: South End Press.

Horowitz, D. (1997). *The Fifties: The Way We Really Were*. Chapel Hill, NC: University of North Carolina Press.

Jeffries, S. (2024). 'John Inman Loved Women, He Just Didn't Sleep with Them'. *The Telegraph*. Retrieved from www.telegraph.co.uk/tv/0/john-inman-sexuality-mr-humphries.

Khubchandani, K. (2023). *Decolonize Drag*. New York: OR Books.

Kings Of The World (2020). 'Drag King History'. KOTW. Retrieved from https://dragkinghistory.com/kotw (accessed June 2025).

Kinsella, S. (2020). 'Otoko no ko Manga and New Wave Crossdressing in the 2000s: A Two-Dimensional to Three-Dimensional Male Subculture', *Mechademia: Second Arc*, *13*(1), 40–56.

Koster, A. (2024). 'Kween Kong On Finding Her Samoan Identity Through Drag & Using Her Influence For Good'. Refinery 29. Retrieved from www.refinery29.com/en-au/kween-kong-interview-my-first-time (accessed June 2025).

Krausz, P. (2003). 'Screening Indigenous Australia: An Overview of Aboriginal Representation in Film'. *Australian Teachers of Media*, 32, 90–96.

Kruger, C. (n.d.). 'Review: "The Wizard of Oz" at A.C.T. (★★★★★)'. TheatreStorm. Retrieved from https://theatrestorm.com/2023/06/08/review-the-wizard-of-oz-at-a-c-t (accessed June 2025).

Laamanen, M., Micheli, M. R., Campana, M., Venkatraman, R., & Duffy, K. (2025). 'Introduction: What are Marketplace Cultures of Drag?'. In Laamanen, M., Micheli, M. R., Campana, M., Venkatraman, R., & Duffy, K. (eds), *Drag as Marketplace*, 1–18. Bristol: Bristol University Press.

Laforteza, E. (2006). 'What a Drag! Filipina/White Australian Relations in *The Adventures of Priscilla, Queen of the Desert*', *Australian Critical Race and Whiteness Studies Association*, 2(2), 1–18.

Lefevre, F. (2021). 'Lip-Syncing for Our Lives: Queering Dissent in Queer & Now a Lip-Sync Spectacular'. In Tiina Rosenberg, T., D'Urso, S. & Winget, A. R. (eds), *The Palgrave Handbook of Queer and Trans Feminisms in Contemporary Performance*, 243–262. Basingstoke: Palgrave Macmillan.

Margaret Thatcher Foundation. (n.d.). 'Release of MT's Private Files for 1982 – Life at No.10'. Retrieved from www.margaretthatcher.org/archive/1982cac7 (accessed June 2025).

McLuhan, M. (1964). *Understanding Media: The Extensions of Man*. New York: McGraw-Hill.

Menchavez, A. (2020). 'Drag Race Queens of Color on Fandom Racism, Visibility and Impact'. GLAAD. Retrieved from https://glaad.org/drag-race-queens-color-fandom-racism-visibility-and-impact (accessed June 2025).

Meta (2022). 'Queens of the Metaverse: The First-Ever Mixed Reality Drag Show'. Retrieved from https://about.fb.com/news/2022/09/queens-of-the-metaverse-the-first-ever-mixed-reality-drag-show (accessed June 2025).

National Film and Sound Archive of Australia (n.d.). 'You and Me by John-Michael Howson and Jeanne Little (1984)'. Retrieved from www.nfsa.gov.au/collection/curated/asset/98988-you-and-me-john-michael-howson-and-jeanne-little (accessed June 2025).

Needham, A. (2007). 'John Inman: A Gay Icon?'. The Guardian. Retrieved from www.theguardian.com/culture/tvandradioblog/2007/mar/08/johninmanagayicon (accessed June 2025).

Parslow, J. (2023). 'Kings, Queens, Monsters, and Things: Digital Drag Performance and Queer Moves in Artificial Intelligence (AI)', *Contemporary Theatre Review*, 33(1–2), 128–148.

Reynolds, D. (2020). 'Black "Drag Race" Stars Urge Fans to "Stop the Racism" in PSA'. Advocate. Retrieved from www.advocate.com/race/2020/9/21/black-drag-race-stars-urge-fans-stop-racism-psa?utm.

Sandhu, A. (2019). 'India's Digital Drag Aunties: Breaking New Ground Wearing Familiar Fashions'. *Dress*, 45(1), 55–73.

Schlutt, M. (2020). 'Spilling Tea with the World's Most Popular Drag Queen Pabllo Vittar'. Kaltblut Magazine. Retrieved from www.kaltblut-magazine.com/spilling-tea-with-the-worlds-most-popular-drag-queen-pabllo-vittar (accessed June 2025).

Sim, B. (2025). 'All the Drag Race Queens on OnlyFans (& What They're Showing)'. Out. Retrieved from www.out.com/drag/drag-race-onlyfans#rebelltitem1 (accessed June 2025).

Skyy, B. A. (2019). 'Our Genderqueer Art: The Work, Life and Art of Del LaGrace Volcano'. Dallas Voice. Retrieved from https://dallasvoice.com/our-genderqueer-art-the-work-life-and-art-of-del-lagrace-volcano (accessed June 2025).

Smith, J. (2011). 'Postcolonial Māori Television? The Dirty Politics of Indigenous Cultural Production', *Continuum*, 25(5), 719–729.

Squillante, L. (2025). 'The Neoliberal "Ru-presentation" of Drag as a Key to Success and Acceptance'. In Laamanen, M., Micheli, M. R., Campana, M., Venkatraman, R., & Duffy, K. (eds), *Drag as Marketplace*, 21–43. Bristol: Bristol University Press.

Stein, K. (2023). 'You Better Work! Drag Queen Performativity and Visibility on# Dragqueen TikTok', *Queer Studies in Media & Popular Culture*, 8(2), 139–157.

Superdrug (n.d.). 'Case Study: Superdrag'. Retrieved from www.superdrugexperience.com/case-studies/superdrag (accessed June 2025).

Sutherland, M., & Wilson, F. (2008). *The Flip Wilson Show*. Detroit, MI: Wayne State University Press.

Te Ara Encyclopedia of New Zealand (n.d.). 'TV Interview with Carmen Rupe, 1975'. Retrieved from https://teara.govt.nz/en/video/47038/tv-interview-with-carmen-rupe-1975 (accessed June 2025).

Tilley, S. (1997; reprint 2025). *Leigh Bowery: The Life and Times of an Icon*. London: Hodder & Stoughton.

Trammel, J. M. (2023). 'Artificial Intelligence for Social Evil: Exploring How AI and Beauty Filters Perpetuate Colorism – Lessons Learned from a Colorism Giant, Brazil'. In Langmia, K. (ed.), *Black Communication in the Age of Disinformation*, 47–64. Basingstoke: Palgrave Macmillan.

Varela Rodríguez, P. (2012). 'Shooting the other: Representations of Aboriginal and Torres Strait Islander masculinities in 21st century Australian cinema' (Master's dissertation, University of Barcelona). Retrieved from: https://diposit.ub.edu/dspace/bitstream/2445/32277/1/Shooting%20the%20Other%20Representations%20of%20Aboriginal%20and%20Torres.pdf (accessed June 2025).

Waugh, T. (2006). *The Romance of transgression in Canada: Queering Sexualities, Nations, Cinemas*. Waterloo, Ontario: Wilfrid Laurier University Press.

CONCLUSION

This chapter concludes the main arguments of *Drag: The Basics*, in the form of a reflection that focuses on the tensions and incoherences of drag cultures today. As authors, we warn against the danger of conformity of the art form in mainstream contexts.

We began this book by noting how drag resists tidy definitions. In the very same way, it refuses neat conclusions. Drag's essence is captured in this resistance and its refusal to be categorised, as that simply limits its scope. Across the histories/herstories, theories, practices, issues, and media landscapes covered in this book, what emerges is not a coherent account of drag, but accounts and case studies interwoven in a tapestry that reveals drag's tensions and loose threads. There is much unfinished work, for drag cultures, communities, and drag studies.

The visibility of drag carries the danger of conformity. As drag has moved from subcultural performance into global media enterprises, certain versions of drag have been sanitised, branded, privileged, and sold back to audiences as entertainment. Glossy television franchises, social media algorithms, and corporate sponsorships have amplified drag's visibility, but at the cost of centring on specific forms that limit this vision. The mainstreaming of drag reveals a contradiction: a form that once thrived on parody and political disruption risks being reabsorbed into the very structures it once mocked.

This is not a nostalgic lament for some imagined 'authentic' drag past. Drag has always been shaped by its contexts and performed in negotiation with the limits of what was possible. The commercialisation of drag is neither entirely new nor entirely disastrous, but it

DOI: 10.4324/9781003431800-5

is a shift that must be recognised and critiqued. Not all visibility is progress; not all mainstreaming is success. It is our hope that this visibility will increase public performances of other drag forms, paying attention to questions of representation and intersectionality.

Drag's internal dynamics are equally complicated. Throughout this book, attention has been given to the ways drag has excluded as much as it has included. Histories/herstories of drag kings, non-binary performers, and performers of colour have often been marginalised in dominant narratives. Despite drag's reputation as a space of gender subversion, problematic portrayals persist in many drag cultures, including misogyny, racism, body conformity, and ableism. Intersectionality is too often invoked as a buzzword rather than practised as a reality. A critical drag future must involve more than a nod towards diversity and inclusion; it must involve structural change.

Activism, too, faces new challenges. In the face of growing legislative attacks against LGBTQ+ communities globally, drag has been repositioned, often unwillingly, as a symbol in broader culture wars. Story hours and local performances have been politicised beyond their immediate intentions as a result of drag panic. Drag is once again being asked to justify itself, just as it has been at various points in its history. Resisting pushback is part of drag's armour, yet activism feels an urgent activity once again. The future of drag is not assured by its current popularity. If anything, the pressures to conform, commercialise, and sanitise will only intensify. Emerging forms of drag, in digital spaces, outside Western frameworks, and in activist movements, will be crucial sites to watch. These forms may resist the conventional forms and formulae that increasingly dominate mainstream drag media.

Looking ahead, undoubtedly, drag will continue to shape-shift alongside broader cultural, technological, and political changes. The growth of digital drag during the pandemic demonstrated drag's adaptability and versatility. However, digital drag also exposes new inequalities, often reinforcing dominant cultural biases. Digital drag may insist on new modes of performance, new languages of resistance, and new possibilities for what drag can be and do.

Throughout this book, a clear pattern has emerged: drag thrives in its complexity and messiness. For us as authors, drag works best when it disrupts rather than conforms. Drag has always been about more than wigs, costumes, and performances; it has been about revealing the instability of the categories that society takes for granted.

To engage seriously with drag is to stay with its discomforts while evaluating the form with both critical attention and care. The task is to recognise drag's contradictions without smoothing them over. We can acknowledge drag's histories without having to romanticise them. We can celebrate its possibilities without ignoring its failures.

Drag's future will not be neat. It will not be uniform. It will not be universally radical or universally regressive. Like gender itself, drag is likely to continue to be a site of struggle, creativity, exclusion, redefinition, and resistance.

The work of drag is not to arrive at a final form. It is to continue moving.

Drag's unfinished nature is not its weakness. It is the condition of its gift.

INDEX

For Product Safety Concerns and Information please contact our EU
representative GPSR@taylorandfrancis.com
Taylor & Francis Verlag GmbH, Kaufingerstraße 24, 80331 München, Germany

www.ingramcontent.com/pod-product-compliance
Lightning Source LLC
Chambersburg PA
CBHW050652270326
41927CB00012B/2994